To: Eugene and Wilda

Happy 60TH Anniversary!

Our friends and friends
of Bob.

Sue and
Chuck Carlson
John 15: 15

FRESH BREAD FOR

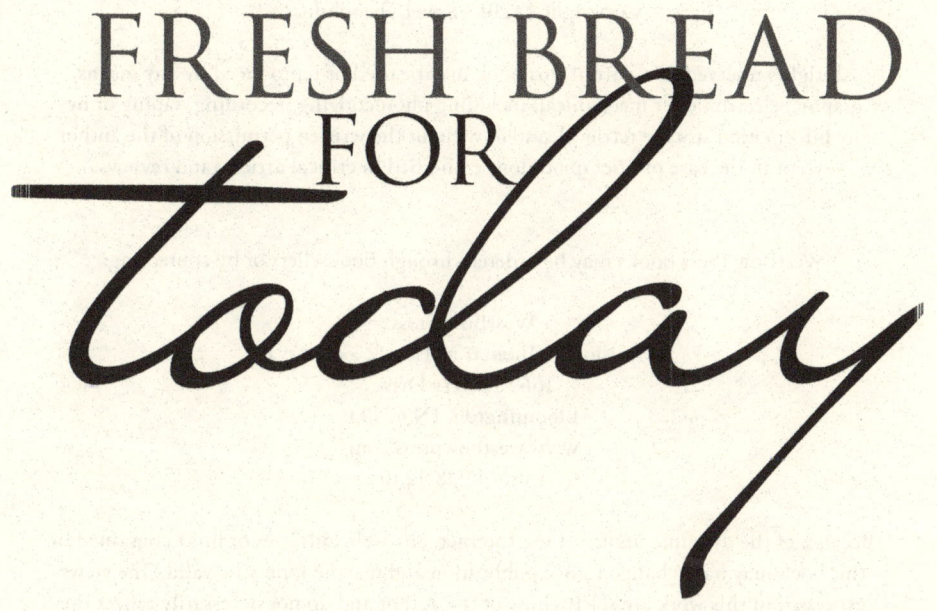

today

REUEL THEOPHILUS

WESTBOW
PRESS®
A DIVISION OF THOMAS NELSON
& ZONDERVAN

WestBow Press books may be ordered through booksellers or by contacting:

WestBow Press
A Division of Thomas Nelson & Zondervan
1663 Liberty Drive
Bloomington, IN 47403
www.westbowpress.com
1 (866) 928-1240

ISBN: 978-1-5127-9329-1 (sc)
ISBN: 978-1-5127-9328-4 (hc)
ISBN: 978-1-5127-9330-7 (e)

Library of Congress Control Number: 2017910544

Print information available on the last page.

WestBow Press rev. date: 08/02/2017

INTRODUCTION

This writing is the result of the encouragement from the men's group that is facilitated each Monday night by Darrell Thompson in his home. These men, in particular, Darrell Thompson and Gary Van Hee, have encouraged me to share what our Father in Heaven has been speaking.

I have had many questions as I have started this writing. Who is the audience? What should I write? How should I proceed? These are just a few of the questions. The most significant point about this endeavor is I know that what I am writing is being given to me by the Holy Spirit. Therefore, I do not own these writings. They are being given to me to edify and encourage my brothers and sisters in Christ.

I have been prompted to use a penname rather than my name, a penname that is both Hebrew (Reuel) and Theophilus (Greek). Reuel is the father-in-law of Moses in the Old Testament and Theophilus is in the New Testament. Both names, Reuel and Theophilus, mean friend of God. Once we receive Jesus Christ as Lord and Savior we are friends of God.

These devotions are intended to be personal between you and Father God. Your Bible, the inspired Word of God, tells you that there is nothing new under the sun. It would be foolish to think these devotional writings are necessarily new or original. Most all of us are products of the things we have learned or experienced. The Bible also tells us we need fresh Bread daily. You must ask Father God to give you the fresh Bread He has prepared. It might be the verse you have literally read a hundred times or even memorized, but this very day as you ask and seek Father God for the fresh Bread He may very well open your eyes to see what you have never seen before in that verse!

You ask, why is this physical tent so important? It is so important because your body is the temple of the Living God. Paul states in Colossians chapter one your Lord Jesus living in you is the hope of glory!

Father God tells you He wants you to be healthy and strong. Therefore, you need His Word because He tells you that you shall not live by physical food alone but every Word that comes from Him.

The purpose in this writing is to encourage and strengthen you as you read and hear from the Lord through the Holy Spirit the fresh Bread you receive on a daily basis. As you read, you will be encouraged and strengthened in your personal reading of God's Word. It is testimony on a daily basis of the faithfulness of your God. He is faithful beyond words! You can trust Him. As you read these brief writings or slices, Father God will reveal Himself in a fresh way and bring life to you in your moment of seeking because He has promised you will find Him when you seek Him!

In Jesus Christ be blessed as you read and receive from Him renewed life and strength. His Word is life to your flesh and strength to your bones. His Word will not return void! Father God has promised and all of His promises are yes and amen in Christ Jesus.

Then I fell down at his feet to worship him, but he [stopped me and] said to me, "You must not do that; I am a fellow servant with you and your brothers and sisters who have and hold the testimony of Jesus. Worship God [alone]. For the testimony of Jesus is the spirit of prophecy [His life and teaching are the heart of prophecy]. **Revelation 19:10 (AMP)**

Here in Revelation nineteen we learn the testimony of our Lord Jesus is the spirit of prophecy. Our Lord Jesus' testimony is that He spoke only what He heard His Father say. As children of God our desire should be to imitate our Lord Jesus because He is the Way. Therefore, the words that are shared are intended to be what I have heard and believed as I read the Word and listen for the Holy Spirit to emphasize and enlighten what to share.

My prayer is eyes, ears, and hearts will be open to hear and receive from the Holy Spirit the Truth that is related in Testimony, here in these pages and brief writings, to the presence of the Living God in our lives! The Testimony of Jesus is He lives! He has risen and He lives in our hearts!

Take, eat, and as you meditate on these words, do it in remembrance of our Lord Jesus Christ and what He has done for you.

FOREWORD

by Evangelist & Pastor David Dodd

John 6:50 says, "This is the bread that comes down from heaven, so that one may eat of it and not die." I remember the first time I ever caught the fragrance of fresh baked bread. You see, I had the terrible misfortune of growing up with the modern convenience of grocery stores with mass-produced breads from various bakeries. My mother didn't bake bread at home but rather would choose and buy a loaf of white bread from the aisle at our local store.

My introduction to fresh bread came as a teen while having dinner in the home of a friend. It was upon entry of the home that I caught a whiff of the most delicious and tantalizing scent that I had ever smelled. It was thick and enticing and it stirred up a physical hunger and whetted my appetite. I wondered what it was that I was smelling. So it was there I got my first whiff of fresh bread, painstakingly homemade and baked. The host mother smiled at my captivation and nodded toward the kitchen table, and there, sitting in a basket and wrapped in linen, was the wonderfully fresh baked bread. I was told this was the tasting loaf, something to nibble on while we waited for the rest of the meal. A slice was cut and handed to me and I took a bite! AMAZING! That first bite was unbelievably good, hot and alone, with no butter to accompany it, was simply the best thing ever! So good! I will never forget this first time experience at a friend's table having fresh bread!

I have a saying and it is this, "My truest friends stir my passion for God." As I sit here writing this foreword, this rings intensely true of my relationship with Chuck Carlson. I would be remiss if I didn't say how much Chuck means to me and to my family; he has been a mentor and a father, an encourager and a teacher, one who will give a hard word of truth on behalf of my personal growth and also one who has shared tears and wept with me in some of my life's deepest sorrow and tragedy. While I could go into great detail and description of the many roles Chuck has played in my life, the one I will stick with for the sake of this writing is as I stated in the first sentence and simply, he is my good, good true friend.

Much like the story above, I will also never forget my first-time experience of having an altogether different Fresh Bread sitting at a well-worn wooden table with Chuck Carlson. It was the summer of 1998 and I was an intern with the student ministries of Calvary Temple church in Auburn, WA. Chuck and Sue kindly hosted me in their home. Chuck and I didn't meet for most of that summer as he was away fishing and I was away at camps and retreats and activities. Somewhere in between the summer activities, our schedules permitted us to run into each other and it was then that I was invited to sit down and talk. It was here that I first saw Fresh Bread at work.

All of us are responsible for living our lives in a manner that glorifies Christ and brings honor to His kingdom. As a Christian, I sense a deep responsibility to live each moment in a way that pleases my Lord. He has placed us on this planet at this time in history for a purpose.

All Christians will be held accountable for what they have done with their time, talent, and treasure. We may come from many and various different backgrounds, but there are three things we can all be certain of: (1) one day we will all be together; (2) time, as we know it, will be no more; and (3) all our work will be judged by fire.

I really believe that it's because of this very line of thinking that our Father God impressed an urgency upon Chuck to embark upon the writing of this book, "Fresh Bread."

I have read this book many times before it was written, as Chuck at his table, would share with me what God was speaking from the Word in that moment. You see, this book is simply one man's relationship and devotion to his God and in turn the revealing of fresh and timeless truths from that relationship. Psalm 34:8 says, "Taste and see that the Lord is good. Oh, the joys of those who take refuge in him!"

Within these pages you are invited into a man's history with His God. This same God impressed upon this man to write and leave this history for those who would happen upon it. It is written differently and out of divine inspiration, because it is a daily conversation with the King of Kings and the Lord of Lords! If you so happen upon it, know this, as you are reading these words you will be pressed into a passionate relationship and from it you will be invited to partake of Fresh Bread given by the hand of God. It will mature you into becoming more and more a friend of God who is loved of God.

PREFACE

This book was written by waiting on the Lord, listening daily for nearly two years and then writing each day what I was hearing. One or two paragraphs and sometimes a page or two, one step at a time, one day at a time, this is the walk as we listen to our Lord Jesus and let Him direct our steps.

There is no substitute for the Bread of Life. The Word of our Lord God is fresh every time we open it and read. We shouldn't go a day without consuming at least one verse. Each Word is God-breathed and is life to us as we take it in and meditate on it. We may need to allow the Holy Spirit to plow up the hard ground of our hearts from time to time so the Word can take root and produce the fruit our Heavenly Father intends for us to produce. His Word tells us His desire for us is to produce much fruit not just some fruit. Let us now take and eat.

1 CREATED FOR HIS GLORY

Everyone who is called by my name, whom I created for my glory, whom I formed and made. **Isaiah 43:7 (NIV)**

For in him all things were created: things in heaven and on earth, visible and invisible, whether thrones or powers or rulers or authorities; all things have been created through him and for him. **Colossians 1:16 (NIV)**

You were created by Him and you were created for Him. You were in His mind from the very beginning. You see this in Genesis when He says, "Let us make man in our own image." Our Heavenly Father established a very personal relationship with Adam and his wife Eve. He would come to the garden to have fellowship with His children. That divine relationship was interrupted by the Serpent, the Devil, when he deceived Eve and led her into sin. Adam was with Eve and he went along with her. Because Adam wasn't deceived, he chose to sin right along with His wife Eve.

This did not surprise our Heavenly Father and from the beginning He initiated His salvation plan for reconciliation and restoration of your relationship with Him through His Son, our Lord Jesus Christ. Our Lord Jesus is the Way, the Truth and the Life. No man comes to the Father but through Him.

$\mathcal{2}$ RELATIONSHIP

The seventeenth chapter of John is Jesus' prayer in the Garden of Gethsemane. In this prayer you can see the heart of our Lord Jesus Christ as He prays to our Father God. What a privilege to listen in on the Son of God talking to His Father. Every word is relevant. You see His relationship with the Father and His relationship with His disciples and you. For you to see and be reassured by God Himself of your personal relationship with Him is beyond words to describe! Yes, understanding that you have life abundant now and forever--"Eternal Life"-- is beyond words!

Now this is eternal life: that they know you, the only true God, and Jesus Christ, whom you have sent. **John 17:3 (NIV)**

Knowing Jesus Christ and Father God is more than knowledge. You can know about God, but do you have a personal relationship with Jesus and the Father? You start by receiving Him (Jesus Christ) as Lord and Savior. Jesus tells you that as you seek Him you will find Him. He is not that hard to find. Jesus answered, "The work of God is this: to believe in the one he has sent." **John 6:29 (NIV)**

You must believe that He is and that He is the rewarder of those who diligently seek Him. Jesus also tells you that you are blessed because you believe even though you haven't seen. This faith comes from hearing the Word. Then His Word tells you, "without faith it is impossible to please Him." You want to be a God pleaser!

Daily you need fresh Bread. You know this because He tells you in His Word, "Desire the sincere milk of the Word that you may grow thereby." This is head knowledge that has moved from your head to your heart. When you daily ask for and receive fresh Bread, just as He taught His disciples to ask for daily bread, You are in relationship with Him.

Acknowledging God in everything you do is entering into the restored relationship with Father God that He has purposed for you, just as Adam and Eve experienced and enjoyed in the Garden of Eden! You can come to Father God anytime anywhere. He is there! He is a friend that stays closer than a brother. He will never leave you or forsake you! You have oneness with Him and with others as you enter into the relationship He has provided for you.

Listen to Jesus' prayer as He includes you and confirms the oneness that you can have in Him! Why would you not say, "Yes! Yes! Yes! Yes!" I say "Yes!" more than once because I want the complete and total victory purchased by the Blood of our Lord and Savior Jesus Christ!

My prayer is not for them alone. I pray also for those who will believe in me through their message, that all of them may be one, Father, just as you are in me and I am in you. May they also be in us so that the world may believe that you have sent me. I have given them the glory that you gave me, that they may be one as we are one—I in them and you in me—so that they may be brought to complete unity. Then the world will know that you sent me and have loved them even as you have loved me. **John 17:20--23 (NIV)**

3 LUKEWARM

I know your deeds, that you are neither cold nor hot. I wish you were either one or the other! So, because you are lukewarm—neither hot nor cold—I am about to spit you out of my mouth. You say, 'I am rich; I have acquired wealth and do not need a thing.' But you do not realize that you are wretched, pitiful, poor, blind and naked. **Revelation 3:15--17 (NIV)**

When you ask the Lord about being lukewarm, the answer may surprise you. Another word for lukewarm is comfortable. You have in all likelihood spent a great deal of your life working to be comfortable. Once you obtain that comfort you don't want to leave it whether it's your warm bed in the morning or your recliner in the evening. Whatever it is, whether you are riding in the car or taking your daily walk, you are comfort conscious.

Wherever or whatever, comfort is involved in some way. As long as you are comfortable, things are good. As long as I am comfortable, there will not be much effort or desire to change. Once there is discomfort then I become fully engaged in trying to restore that comfort. As a dog returns to its vomit, so fools repeat their folly. **Proverbs 26:11 (NIV)**

Spiritual discomfort comes when our Heavenly Father wants to work or bring change or transformation into our lives. When we become comfortable spiritually, we are in danger of being lukewarm. Jesus' message is, "I have come to seek and to save that

which is lost. I have come to make you uncomfortable." If you are not uncomfortable you will not change. Everyone, including me, wants to be comfortable. I do not like change. I work to be comfortable.

I love you, Lord. I thank You for speaking to me and putting me in an uncomfortable position so I can hear Your voice. I need to understand that in all I am going through You are working all of it for my good and my benefit. It may not be and most likely isn't a feel-good position. It most often will be uncomfortable. Our Heavenly Father had to take the children of Israel out of Egypt where even in adverse conditions they had become comfortable. They came out of Egypt into discomfort for a season.

4 BE CAREFUL WHAT YOU SAY

If I am having problems, I need to consider what I am listening to and what I am speaking. Am I speaking life or I am speaking death? The tongue has the power of life and death, and those who love it will eat its fruit. **Proverbs 18:21 (NIV)**

We are products of what has been spoken over us. I am what God says I am. Examples of words spoken over me that encouraged me: "I am proud of you, son," and "Chuck, I have got your back."

Faith comes by hearing and hearing by the Word.

I need to speak words of life over myself and all those around me.

5 GOD'S GARDEN

Some of you either will or are planting a garden this year. Before we plant we must prepare the soil for planting. We break up the hard ground and the clods (clumps of dirt) so that the soil is fine and soft. Then we plant the seeds at the proper depth in the soil we have readied for planting. If it is dry, we sprinkle the planted soil. We may even place a scarecrow in the garden to keep the birds from coming to eat the seeds or young sprouts as they start to break through the soil to gain access to the sunlight. We also do all we can to keep the slugs, gophers, and cutworms from feasting on the seeds and then the young plants as they sprout. Are you expecting?

You should be expecting. How does the farmer wait? He plants the seeds, weeds, and waters and waits expecting the crop. Start making preparations for receiving the promises of Father God.

Therefore be patient, brethren, until the coming of the Lord. See how the farmer waits for the precious fruit of the earth, waiting patiently for it until it receives the early and latter rain. You also be patient. Establish your hearts, for the coming of the Lord is at hand. **James 5:7-8**

In due season God will bring to pass the desires of your heart. Habakkuk tells us the vision may tarry but we are to wait expectantly. The vision will not be one second late.

Don't let bad news discourage you. Father God will do what He has promised. Faithful is He who has called you who will also do it.

6 MARKS

Often when someone gets hit or falls we hear, "That will leave a mark!" Everything we do will leave a mark. Some marks are visible and some cannot be seen but they can be felt.

As I go through my day what kind of marks am I leaving? Can you see where I have been? What have I done to those and myself around me? My actions and my words leave marks.

Some marks leave scars. Some scars are visible and some cannot be seen. Often the unseen scars have pain that doesn't seem to go away. What can be done that will help and heal these marks? The first thing I need to do is to give all my scars to my Lord Jesus. I need to believe and receive His Words of Life to me. His Words are life and healing.

Receive in the Greek is *Lambano*. It is an active verb that means to aggressively take. I must take what God has given me and act upon it. My Lord Jesus has given it to me. There is no question He wants me to take it.

Before I can help others I must be a well person. Otherwise I will hurt those around me. I will leave a lot of ugly marks.

He himself bore our sins in his body on the cross, so that we might die to sins and live for righteousness; by his wounds you have been healed. **1 Peter 2:24**

I am forgiven and made whole spiritually and physically. I need each day, as I begin my day and as I go through my day, to keep

His Words before me. With the help of the Holy Spirit, I can let the love of Christ control my actions and my tongue so that my actions will leave no ugly or hurtful marks. Instead those around me will be strengthened and encouraged!

Father God, I can only do this with You and through You. Help me this day to make only marks that will honor You! In Jesus' Name I ask and believe.

7 THE WORD

Our Father in Heaven tells us and has demonstrated what He has spoken, that He will spare nothing to help us. "How?" you say. Listen to this and I believe you will see! If while we were sinners He spared not His only Son that we might have eternal life how much more will He do for us now that we are His children? Why then do we go everywhere but to Him when we have a need? Could our problem be we don't believe?

In order to believe we need to know our Lord Jesus Christ and Father God through relationship with Him. That relationship comes through knowing Him through His Word. We need to hear His Word as we read! Read at times, if possible, out loud so you can hear! Faith comes by hearing and hearing by His Word. There is no substitute. I need to daily read the Word!

The Book of Proverbs is a wonderful book to feed upon. Billy Graham has read Proverbs monthly for years. A chapter a day will get you through Proverbs pretty much every month since there are thirty-one chapters. The Word of God is priceless and the Word is LIFE! YES, LIFE!

Before you read the verses that follow from Proverbs four, pray with me this prayer: *Father God, open my eyes to see and let my heart receive the Word You are about to speak to me. In Jesus' Name I pray, Amen.*

My child, pay attention to what I say. Listen carefully to my words. Don't lose sight of them. Let them penetrate deep into your heart, for they bring life to those who find them, and healing to their whole body. **Proverbs 4:20--21 (NLT)**

8 BODY MINISTRY

First Corinthians twelve tells us about the gifts of the Holy Spirit and the Body of Christ. As believers, we are the Body of Christ and our Lord Jesus is our Head. We are all different parts of the Body. Each of us is necessary for the other. Our Lord Jesus in John seventeen prayed that we would be ONE even as He is one with the Father.

The Father has given us, the Body, spiritual gifts. He wants His Body (us) well and strong. The purpose of the gifts is so that we can encourage one another and build each other up!

Our Father knows what we need even before we ask. Why then do have to ask? He tells us we have not because we don't ask. When we ask we are saying, "Father, I believe you so I am asking." Believing and asking, we receive! When we believe and ask our Father, the need we are praying for is taken care of at that very moment.

Our God is not deaf and His arm has not been shortened. It is not based on any feeling or anything other than His Word. His Word will not return void. He gives us title for our miracle that has been paid for by our Lord Jesus' blood and stripes. When we ask and believe, we are given our title deed and we will receive and take possession of that miracle!

Yesterday the Holy Spirit spoke three words very clearly, "Peace, be still!" This is His Word to us right now. Every situation we are facing, no matter what it is, these three words are life to that situation or circumstance we are facing. We need to understand that our Father God is bringing His peace to our needs. We need to understand. We are the Body with our Lord Jesus as our Head and we have the Prince of Peace with us at all times. We can't lose! We are more than conquerors in Him!

A spiritual gift is given to each of us so we can help each other. **First Corinthians 12:7 (NLT)**

9 SEED AND SOWING

The kind of seed you sow will determine the fruit you harvest. If you sow a seed of corn, you will harvest generally one or two ears of corn. If you sow a tomato seed, you will harvest perhaps as many as fifty tomatoes. What we sow determines what we harvest.

If I want faith, I need to sow the Word of God in my heart. Faith comes by hearing and hearing by the Word. What do I want? God's Word tells me if I want it I must ask for it. Jesus said, "You have not because you ask not. Ask and you shall receive."

When I ask I must also believe that I will receive. Faith will overrule my senses and allow me to walk on the water. My Lord Jesus has bid me to come, and in spite of the waves around me, I will walk to Him and be safe!

Some reading this are in the middle of the storm! Waves, overwhelming waves, are all around! There is nothing to stand on or rest on. Pains, sick feelings, headaches, overwhelming situations, lack of finances, loss of work, loved ones who are ill, and the list goes on. These waves and winds will cause you to sink before you can get to Jesus if the Devil has his way.

The good news is our Lord Jesus has defeated the Devil and gives us the victory. The Word of our Lord Jesus makes the difference in all of these situations we face. Just as Peter cried out, we need to cry out, "Lord, save me!" Jesus rescued Peter and He will rescue us and calm the waves. Our Lord Jesus will never leave us or forsake us. He will make a way for us in every situation and circumstance. Remember He has bid us to come to Him. He will never turn us away.

Believe with me right now. Together we believe and ask, "Lord Jesus help!" This very instant! Jesus has you! You have made it to Him. He now holds you and you are safe! This is what I hear, "PEACE, BE STILL!" I believe you hear it too! The peace of God which passes all understanding shall keep your heart and your mind though Christ Jesus. The joy of the Lord is your strength.

10 THE WORK OF GOD

Jesus answered and said to them, "This is the work of God, that you believe in Him whom He sent." **John 6:29**

Who does the work? I have had difficulty with this. I think I have to do the work. The Word of our Father is very clear. Father God does the work. My part is to believe He will do what He has promised. The quicker I understand He does the work and I am to believe, the quicker things will get better for me!!!

When I believe and let Him have the situation, I will have peace. I will be calm and not get upset when the car next to me cuts me off! I pray this will be true! These little foxes must also be dealt with!

Whatever the crisis that comes my way, my first reaction needs to be to believe. My cry needs to be, "Father, help!" I trust You, Father God, and Your Word to me is, "Be still and know that I am God." He continues to speak, "My peace I give to you, not as the world gives." This peace, the Peace of God, passes all understanding and will keep my heart and my mind through Christ Jesus.

My prayer is, "Father, help me to believe!" My Father in Heaven is the Creator of the universe and everything in it! Nothing is too hard for Him! Nothing, that's right, nothing is too hard for our God. He will do the work! Why? Because I believe and I believe you will join me in believing! All unbelief has to go in Jesus' Name.

Be gone! Amen! Put your trust in God! Don't be afraid. My Father tells me, "Be strong and courageous."

Stand in the middle of the crisis believing and you will see the deliverance of the Lord!

11 TODAY'S SLICE

Romans 10:8 tells us that the Word is near us even in our mouth. Psalm 103:5 tells us that our Father God satisfies our mouth with good things so that our youth is renewed like the eagles.

This is a most wonderful Word for us this day! It satisfies like no other food! It is directly from the King's table! Our Lord God has handed us food that is the very "Breath of Life." This fresh Bread is directly from His mouth. With this Word nothing is impossible! Our Lord God is saying, "Let your eyes be opened this very moment. Receive! Receive! Receive! Receive!"

Father God is saying, "You are mine! Mine! Yes, you are my child! I have saved you and there is nothing I will not do in your behalf now you are mine! I will supply all your needs. No weapon formed against you will prosper. I am the Lord who heals you. I am your defender. Nothing can separate you from my love!"

Faith comes by hearing and hearing by the Word of God! Read this brief word out loud. Your spiritual ears need to hear it. Hearing it you will receive directly from our Father a measure of faith. This is not a formula; it is a Word from our Father God. In obedience to His Word, then read this Word again out loud. He wants us to speak to the difficulty whatever you are facing. Health, financial, struggle in relationship, job, whatever it is, in Jesus' Name, situation, be made whole. Situation, be made whole in the mighty name of Jesus Christ, move and be gone! Amen!

Having done this, believing, stand still, wait and you will see the victory! Our Father God's Word will not return void.

12 ANOTHER SLICE

Father, You have a fresh slice of Bread for us today. You have told us to ask. Therefore we are asking, Give us today our daily Bread. You are our Heavenly Father so we know You will not give us a stone. Then He touched their eyes, saying, "According to your faith let it be to you." **Matthew 9:29**

We have been this close to answered prayer many times before. Why haven't we received? From the Bread given us we see that believing and faith are essential to receiving our answer. What else could keep us from receiving?

Are we willing to wait for our Lord to answer? I was reading in Nehemiah the first chapter. Nehemiah asked God to go to Jerusalem. He was a cupbearer, slave to the king hundreds of miles away. This required a miracle for him to be able to go. As I continued to read I learned that four months later he got his answer. I thought, "Wow, four months!" In my spirit I heard this, "Yes, Chuck, many times I would have answered your prayers but you didn't wait!"

When we pray believing, we must be convinced that our Father will do what He has promised. All of His promises are yes and amen in Christ Jesus, He is not deaf, and His arm has not been shortened that He cannot reach us. This is truth. What our Father has spoken He will do. His Word will not return void! I believe the fresh slice for us today is that as we have asked and as we have believed, we will receive. Stand still in the Lord and wait. We will see and we will receive! Don't panic! Wait on the Lord. He will come through for us.

13 FACING A CRISIS

What to do? What to do? Overwhelming feelings sweep over us at times. We are caring for a loved one and there seems to be no relief or there is not enough money to pay the bills.

First of all, I need to stop! Where is this coming from? Am I afraid? If there is even the slightest bit of fear, I know what is happening is not from Father God. He has not given me a spirit of fear. His Word tells me His good thoughts towards me are more numerous than the sands of the sea. Wow, that is better already!

He also tells me that I should run to Him! That's run, not walk! The name of the Lord is a strong tower and the righteous run into it and are safe! **Proverbs 18:10**

Now I am safe in the tower and He tells me what to do. Sometimes He tells me that I need to choose differently. Sometimes He tells me to speak to the situations I am facing. What do I say? He tells me to speak His Word. His Word is near me even in my mouth. I can say to the situation, "Situation, you have to change or you have to leave. I do not own you. You are not mine, leave."

Most of these things are from the Enemy. The Enemy wants to kill, steal and destroy. He is defeated and our Lord Jesus has given us the power and authority to send the Enemy on His way. Father God tells us not to give the Enemy any place in our lives. That's right, kick him out! Submit ourselves to Father God and resist the Devil and he has to flee! Be gone in Jesus' Name!

14 A CHILD SHALL LEAD THEM

And a little child shall lead them. **Isaiah 11:6** But Jesus called them to Him and said, "Let the little children come to Me, and do not forbid them; for of such is the kingdom of God. **Luke 18:16**

In 2004 I had the privilege of going to Tanzania, Africa, and visiting a school and orphanage as it was beginning. Pastors Glorious and Josephine Shoo, prompted by the Holy Spirit, began this ministry. Today they are caring for more than 500 children. I can still hear the children singing, "I am walking in a miracle life!" I will never be the same.

I have had the privilege of seeing the children pray for each other while in Tanzania. I was most blessed to have them pray for me while I was there. I pray that many of you will have like opportunities. We all can by supporting those who are serving these children.

They are an encouragement to us. We are the Body of Christ and when one of us is hurting we are all hurting. Let's listen. Our Father tells us to pray for one another according to His Word. Our Father's Word tells us to lay hands on the sick and they will recover. That's right, they will get well. We have God's Word on it and His Word will not return void. Do not be afraid. Our loving Father will do His part when we do ours.

15 CHOICES

Every day brings its choices to us. I am living today with the choices I made yesterday. I will live tomorrow with the choices I make today. Some choices have more significance than others do. The choices that affect me long term are the most important choices. As God's children we need to understand our choices make a difference. What I am going through right now is to a large extent the result of choices I made yesterday and the day before that. Every choice has a consequence.

The Bible is my choice for living. Do I want to know what it says? If I answer yes, what am I doing about learning what it says? Am I feeding myself or am I totally dependent on others to feed me? How often am I feeding? If I am only feeding once or twice a week, how strong can I expect to be? Do I ask for my Father God's daily Bread He has prepared for me? To eat daily the Father's Bread is life to me!

And if it seems evil to you to serve the LORD, choose for yourselves this day whom you will serve, whether the gods which your fathers served that were on the other side of the River, or the gods of the Amorites, in whose land you dwell. But as for me and my house, we will serve the LORD. **Joshua 24:15**

16 PLANTING--SOWING

The kinds of seeds we sow determine the crop that will be produced. We harvest more than we sow and we harvest later than we sow. We also have to care for what we sow. We have to weed, cultivate, and water what we sow. We also have to wait for what we sow to produce a crop.

My Grandpa Heaton planted the Word of God in my life more than seventy years ago. The first reading I did was when Grandpa would have me read from the Gospel of John. He gave me his approval, smiling as I read, "In the beginning was the Word. And the Word was with God and the Word was God. All things were made by Him and without Him nothing was made that was made…" I have not forgotten these Words. This very day they are life to me. All of us, like my Grandpa, are sowing seeds every day. I want to sow seeds like my Grandpa.

Be not deceived; God is not mocked: for whatsoever a man soweth, that shall he also reap. For he that soweth to his flesh shall of the flesh reap corruption; but he that soweth to the Spirit shall of the Spirit reap life everlasting. And let us not be weary in well doing: for in due season we shall reap, if we faint not. **Galatians 6:7--9 (KJV)**

17 FRESH BREAD

The children of Israel were provided for daily in their forty years wandering in the desert. Father God gave them manna every morning. Whatever they would eat for the day they would collect in the morning. If they gathered more than for one day, the extra would spoil. Father God gave it specifically for them for that day and that day only. Only the day before the Sabbath could they gather enough for two days so that they could rest during the Sabbath.

There was always enough manna. Every day the manna was fresh. Father God, in His Word to me, tells me He has recorded this account for my benefit. What does Father God want me to understand from this? As we ask Father God for the answer, He begins to show us in His Word that our Lord Jesus is the Bread of Life. His Word continues to tell us we shall not live by bread alone but every Word that proceeds from the mouth of God. Then Jesus tells us in the model for prayer to pray for daily bread. What our Father God is telling me is that He has fresh Bread for me every day! There is nothing like the smell of fresh baked bread! The Word fresh every day is even better! The thing I am beginning to see is that the supply is endless! Creator God, my heavenly Father, wants to give me a fresh Word every day that is beyond my words! Wow! To hear directly from the Source of Life! Yes, my God is speaking directly to you and me! Just to hear the word Son or Daughter from the Father gives me holy goose bumps even as I write this! Yes, our Father is speaking.

Listen! Listen! Be still! I believe this is what you will hear! "You are my beloved child! I love You with and everlasting love!"

"Herein is love, not that we loved God, but that he loved us, and sent his Son to be the propitiation for our sins. Beloved, if God so loved us, we ought also to love one another." **First John 4:10--11**

18 AN EXAMPLE FOR US

What happened to the children of Israel and the way they responded to the promises of our Heavenly Father has been recorded for us to learn. What was it they continuously did? They complained. They were caught up in what they were experiencing and felt. They were very uncomfortable. When I am uncomfortable, without the Holy Spirit and the Word of God, my natural tendency is to complain.

Our Heavenly Father's will for me, no matter how uncomfortable I am, is to give thanks! If I continue to complain, I am rejecting my Heavenly Father's Word to me. Without vision I will perish. God's Word is my spiritual vision or sight. As I give thanks, the Word in Philippians four tells me I will receive the peace of God. All of the promises of God are yes and amen in Christ Jesus. However, I will not receive them unless I speak life and stop complaining.

In every situation [no matter what the circumstances] be thankful and continually give thanks to God; for this is the will of God for you in Christ Jesus. **First Thessalonians 5:18 (AMP)**

Now these things happened to them as an example and warning [to us]; they were written for our instruction [to admonish and equip us], upon whom the ends of the ages have come. **First Corinthians 10:11(AMP)**

19 TESTIMONY

For I am persuaded, that neither death, nor life, nor angels, nor principalities, nor powers, nor things present, nor things to come, Nor height, nor depth, nor any other creature, shall be able to separate us from the love of God, which is in Christ Jesus our Lord. **Romans 8:38--39**

The love of God is beyond words and writing to describe. Yet I know the love of God reached me at the lowest point of my life. At twenty years of age I was in my second year of Bible school and I tried to save the world. I shared what I had, preached and prayed and pretty much forgot about eating. At 118 pounds, I had a nervous breakdown. Even in that condition, the battle for life and death was still being fought in my mind. Satan, our accuser, does not and will never fight fairly. He convinced me that everyone, including my Father God, had forsaken me. He momentarily convinced me that this lie was true. I tried to take my life. In the process of dying I heard this, "Nothing can separate you from my love."

I knew this verse in Romans and I cried out, "Help me to undo what I have done. I want to live!" The next three months the battle for my life was intense, but my Lord and my God was doing the fighting for me. It was somewhat like I was in the grandstand watching this battle. There was confinement in a maximum security cell, electroshock treatment, and this word from my doctor as I left the hospital, "Chuck, if you ever want to get well, you should never

set foot inside a church again." I was healed while I was in the hospital. I know, I know my God, our God is real.

There is a lot more to this story but that is not what Father God wants me to share. Our battles are in the mind. Our Bible tells us as a man thinks so is he. Be transformed by the renewing of your mind.

Someone reading this needs to know that Father God is our HOPE. He is eternal and therefore HOPE is eternal! Don't give up! Satan is a liar! "Nothing, nothing, nothing can separate you from the love of God in Christ Jesus." God's plan has and always will be life and that life is abundant!

20 MY MIND

For we are God's fellow workers; you are God's field, you are God's building. According to the grace of God which was given to me, as a wise master builder I have laid the foundation, and another builds on it. But let each one take heed how he builds on it. For no other foundation can anyone lay than that which is laid, which is Jesus Christ. **First Corinthians 3:9--11**

When we believe in our heart and confess with our mouth that Jesus Christ is our Lord and Savior, we are saved according to Father God's Word to us. At this very moment our foundation basis for life is Jesus Christ. He is the One who now works in us through His Holy Spirit. The Holy Spirit lives in us –you and me! We are the Temple of the Living God. Yes, the Holy God, our God, now lives in us. "In Him," our Bible tells us, "We live and move and have our being!" We are in relationship with Father God Himself.

First Peter tells us, "We are holy even as He is holy!" This is hard for our natural man to accept and we initially may say, "No, this can't be!" But Father God wants us to know and come into the understanding of who we are in Christ Jesus! We are a new creation! Old things are passed away. The Word of our Father is so good! He tells us. But as it is written, Eye hath not seen, nor ear heard, neither have entered into the heart of man, the things which God hath prepared for them that love him. **First Corinthians 2:9**

He tells me who I am. Receiving this Word from my Father God, I begin to understand I am everything He says I am. His creative Word has made me a new creation!

I submit myself to my Father God so that He can build on the foundation the building He wants to build. Anything I would try to build on this foundation will burn and perish but the building I allow Him to build will stand and bring glory to my Lord and Savior Jesus Christ! I surrender all. All to Him I owe. He that has begun a good work in me will complete that work! My body is the temple of the Living God. You, my brother and sister, are also the temple of the Living God! Together we are the Body of Christ! We are holy even as He is holy! How do we know? The Bible tells us so!

21 BELIEVE, BELIEVE, BELIEVE, BELIEVE

But without faith it is impossible to please Him, for he who comes to God must believe that He is, and that He is a rewarder of those who diligently seek Him. **Hebrews 11:6**

What might be the most important thing Jesus wanted for His disciples? Would it not also be that if He wanted it for His disciples, He might also want it for you and me? How is it we know what those we love and care about want? Unless we have relationship with those we love and care about, we don't know. Father God wants relationship with you and me so much He spared not His own Son while we were yet sinners to have relationship with us. Oh, how much He cares for you and me! More than we can comprehend! Now that we are His children, how much more will He do for us who love Him and are called according to His purpose!

Yet, what am I doing to respond to Him? Knowing Him and His Son Jesus Christ is life, yes, life eternal! I know Him through reading His Word and listening to Him as He speaks to me through His Word and His presence in my life. I must have His Word. It is my spiritual sight. I have no vision without His Word. As I begin to see and begin to gain understanding, I am hearing Him say what He wants. He is saying, "Yes, what I want is for you to believe. Believe all I have spoken to you!" The word believe is used more than two hundred times in the New Testament. In the Gospel of John it is used eighty-five times.

The disciples struggled with believing. Once we cross over the River of Unbelief and stand in the Land of Belief there is transformation! We begin to become everything our Father in Heaven and Lord Jesus Christ desire for us to become! Father God, I believe! I believe! I need more of You. and the source for me to receive more of You is Your Word!

$\mathcal{22}$ VICTORY

Let us listen to Jesus in His prayer to Father God. And the glory which You gave Me I have given them, that they may be one just as We are one: I in them, and You in Me; that they may be made perfect in one, and that the world may know that You have sent Me, and have loved them as You have loved Me. **John 17:22--23**

This oneness will show the world that we are His disciples! Why then is there so much disagreement among those of us who believe that Jesus Christ is Lord? Should we not be seeking the Lord to enter into the oneness Jesus asked for in His prayer? Jesus prayed for it. It must be His will. Oneness was overwhelmingly evident in the body of believers in Acts. Over and over we read, "They were in one accord."

I believe Father God will tell us as we ask Him. Here is a verse to think about in this regard. Woe to those who are wise in their own eyes, and prudent in their own sight!, **Isaiah 5:21**

I know the enemy does not want this to happen. Now hear this! The enemy is defeated! You, Lord Jesus, are greater! It is time for the enemy to be given notice! We believe and we will receive what You have prayed for!

Lord Jesus, You promised that if I surrender You will do your part in me. I can't change anyone else. I surrender to You. I believe

I will see the unity that You prayed for! I also believe that there are many, many, many, many, and, yes, many who will also surrender and believe! Even so let it be! Lord Jesus, let it be! Today, yes, this very day, we have victory in Jesus, our Lord and Savior!

23 MIRACLE

When asking to see a miracle, the Holy Spirit says, "Take a look in a mirror!" You are looking at a miracle. It took a miracle to hang the stars in space, but when He saved your soul, it took a miracle of love and grace! Praise the Lord! I praise you because I am fearfully and wonderfully made; your works are wonderful, I know that full well. **Psalm 139:14 (NIV)**

24 EMOTIONS

Some would look on any visible emotion as a weakness. Some have been taught that visible tears are a weakness. That is a lie straight from the pit of Hell! Jeremiah was known as the Weeping Prophet, and Jesus wept.

When you hurt we all hurt. We need to understand and see. We are the Body of Christ. Our Lord Jesus Himself is our Head! He is our comfort and strength. The Name of the Lord is a strong tower and the righteous (that's you and me) run into it and are safe! Now that we are in Him, sorrow and mourning have to flee away because our Father God is our comfort and strength. He is pouring out His unspeakable joy full of glory over our heads.

It is morning. The SON is shining! The night has passed! We are in His marvelous light! JOY has come this day to you and me! Let us rejoice and give HIM the sacrifice of our praise! Praise the Lord! Our JOY is based on His Word! In the light there is no darkness! We are in the Light! Our Lord Jesus is the Light! We are in Him!

For His anger is but for a moment, His favor is for life; Weeping may endure for a night, But joy comes in the morning. **Psalm 30:5**

25 RIGHT THINKING

Every thought needs to be taken captive! The battle is in the mind! As a man thinks in his heart, so is he! Do you ever have a strange thought enter your mind? You might have this happen even when you are sitting in church. If the thought is strange, why take ownership of it? My problem comes if I take ownership of the weird thought. This thought most likely is one the enemy has initiated and he wants me to accept it as mine. I am to take this thought captive.

As a Christian, I have been given the mind of Christ. The battlefield is my mind. The Holy Spirit gives me discernment. I submit myself to Father God in my mind and tell that strange thought to go! Yes, submit myself to God and resist the Devil, and he has to take flight! Anything that is not of Christ has to go! I am everything my Father God says I am! Victory in Jesus! This is my song, praising my Savior all the day long!

Casting down arguments and every high thing that exalts itself against the knowledge of God, bringing every thought into captivity to the obedience of Christ. **Second Corinthians 10:5**

For as he thinks in his heart, so is he. "Eat and drink!" he says to you, But his heart is not with you. **Proverbs 23:7**

For "who has known the mind of the Lord that he may instruct Him?" But we have the mind of Christ. **First Corinthians 2:16**

And do not be conformed to this world, but be transformed by the renewing of your mind, that you may prove what is that good and acceptable and perfect will of God. **Romans 12:2**

26 IN HIS PRESENCE

And it came to pass, when Moses entered the tabernacle, that the pillar of cloud descended and stood at the door of the tabernacle, and the Lord talked with Moses. All the people saw the pillar of cloud standing at the tabernacle door, and all the people rose and worshiped, each man in his tent door. So the Lord spoke to Moses face to face, as a man speaks to his friend. And he would return to the camp, but his servant Joshua the son of Nun, a young man, did not depart from the tabernacle. **Exodus 33:9--11**

There were an estimated one million five hundred thousand men and women over the age of twenty who came out of Egypt led by Moses. The personal relationship Moses had with Father God was such that the Bible tells us the Glory of the Lord was radiated on Moses' face so much so that the people asked him to keep his face covered. These adults would stay in their tents and worship. They did not desire to be any closer to God.

Yet the young man Joshua chose to continually be in God's presence. He wanted to listen to God and Moses as they communed. He wanted to be in the presence of the Lord and be there in the daytime when the pillar of the cloud was over the tabernacle. He also wanted to be there in the night when the pillar of fire was present (when God Himself was present).

What does this say to me? It says I can be as close to God as I want and I can have as much of God as I want! Joshua made a

choice as a young man to be as close to God as possible. This choice resulted in a close relationship like Moses with God. He became God's man with the people of Israel. He was only one of two men over the age of twenty when they came out of Egypt that went into the Promised Land! God's will was all of 603,550 men would go in but only two of those received the promise! Joshua made a verbal declaration that he and his family would serve the Lord! Continuing to speak, he said to the people of Israel, "CHOOSE YOU THIS DAY WHOM YOU WILL SERVE!"

27 BELIEVE

Jesus rebuked His disciples after the resurrection when He appeared to them in the upper room having their pity party after the crucifixion. Why did He rebuke them? He rebuked them because they didn't believe the testimony of the witnesses who had seen Jesus alive. These witnesses told the disciples Jesus had risen and was alive. The disciples didn't believe. Jesus tells us to do the work of God we need to believe! Jesus answered them, "This is the work of God, that you believe in him whom he has sent." **John 6:29**

Why do we over-complicate this Word? We need to come as a little child to our Lord Jesus, for He has told us, "Such is the Kingdom of God," when we come to Him as children. We are also told to believe that He is and that He is the rewarder of those who diligently seek Him. Father, I am praying right now our eyes would be open and hearts would be tender towards you so we can receive all of Your Word! Let us seek you and Your glory and no longer be men pleasers, but God pleasers. I believe You and I confess my belief in You and Your Word.

I ask for Your strength to walk in Your power and Your glory according to Your Word. We are Your ambassadors and You have given us Your authority. Be glorified, and in the reading of this Your Word, let Your people see and be healed as they read and receive. Yes, receive in Jesus' Name, be made whole this very moment!

Healing in the Name of Jesus! To God be the glory both now and forever, Amen!

When Jesus had said these things, He departed and hid Himself from them. Though he had done so many signs before them, they still did not believe in Him, so that the word spoken by the prophet Isaiah might be fulfilled: "Lord, who has believed what he heard from us, and to whom has the arm of the Lord been revealed?" Therefore they could not believe. For again Isaiah said, "He has blinded their eyes and hardened their heart, lest they see with their eyes, and understand with their heart, and turn, and I would heal them." Isaiah said these things because he saw his glory and spoke of him. Nevertheless, many even of the authorities believed in him, but for fear of the Pharisees they did not confess it, so that they would not be put out of the synagogue; for they loved the glory that comes from man more than the glory that comes from God. **John 12:36--43**

$\mathcal{28}$ APPROVAL

Am I now trying to win the approval of human beings, or of God? Or am I trying to please people? If I were still trying to please people, I would not be a servant of Christ. **Galatians 1:10 (NIV)**

All of us want to be approved. Rejection quite simply hurts. A couple of questions then come to mind. From whom do we want approval? What are we doing to get approval? And as I write this, another question comes to mind. Am I honest with my answers to the first two questions?

To get to the first question's answer I must determine who is most important in my life. I want Father God to be most important in my life, then my wife, family, and friends. Then I need to, with God's help through the Holy Spirit, make certain that my actions support this order of priority. When I get this priority out of order, I need to let the Holy Spirit get me back on track. My approval from others has to come second to approval from Father God. This is a struggle because it requires faith. Approval from those around may seem more tangible and almost immediate. Father God's approval requires faith because His Word says, "Without faith it is impossible to please Him."

What do we do for approval and to be noticed? Sometimes it is the way we dress, the stories we tell, the things we do for others, the games we play, and even have a Facebook page. None of these things are bad in and of themselves, but what we need to determine

is our priority in doing them. Is my priority to seek God and love Him? His Word tells me if I love Him I will also love my family and neighbors and, yes, I will even love myself, because He tells me if I don't know how to love myself I can't love anyone else. I also must have faith in Him. In order to have faith, I must have and read His Word, because faith comes by hearing and hearing by the Word. His Word tells me the Way to Him is through His Son, the Lord Jesus Christ.

The wonderful thing is when I understand God's way through His Son Jesus Christ, I come to the Father and He sees Jesus in me. Just as He said when Jesus came up out of the water when John baptized Him, "This is my beloved Son in whom I am well pleased!" Father God says to you and me, beloved sons and daughters, "NOW HEAR THIS. I AM WELL PLEASED!"

This should change everything for us. You may even want to start dancing! This is where it's at! This is real! You and I are beloved sons and daughters of Father God, Creator God, Omnipotent God, the only True and Living God, the only One that matters, the Alpha and Omega, the I AM. Yes, we are approved! We have approval! We can be ourselves in Him. We are set free to be real with those around us.

29 THIS IS SERIOUS

I have a great-nephew who when he was around five years old would often say, "Now this is very serious." With that introduction, I would ask this question, "What happens every time we hear the Word of God?" I believe one of two things happen. First, our heart is open to the Word of God and we are edified and built up in the faith. Hebrews tells us, "Faith comes by hearing and hearing by the Word." Or our heart is hardened and we just passively sit there. We have heard this Word before. We wonder how many times do we have to hear the same Word?

The Word of God is like a plow. It will go as deep as we let it go. In farming, to run the plow at the same depth every year will result in what is called hardpan. Basically, continuing to plow that way creates a rock-like condition. This condition prevents nutrients in the soil and moisture from nourishing the seed when it is planted. The crops planted without breaking up the hardpan will be poor! What needs to be done is mechanically set the plow to go deeper. The hardpan is broken up and the seed is nourished and the crops flourish.

When we commit ourselves every time we hear the Word of God and allow the Holy Spirit to go as deep in our hearts as He wants to go, we will be transformed. Jesus says, "Father, sanctify my disciples (includes us) through Thy truth, Thy Word is truth." He was saying with this thought in mind, "Plow up their hearts! Let there be much fruit in their lives!" I believe this is what the Lord is saying to us, "This is serious!"

The Lord is saying to the men of Judah and Jerusalem, Plow up the hardness of your hearts; otherwise the good seed will be wasted among the thorns. **Jeremiah 4:3 (TLB)**

30 BELIEVING

Jesus' disciples were devastated after the crucifixion of our Lord Jesus Christ. Basically hiding and afraid, they did not believe the testimony of the witnesses who had seen Jesus alive after the resurrection. Initially the two Marys reported that Jesus was alive, and for us, we know there were more than 500 who saw Jesus before He ascended back to heaven.

After that, he appeared to more than five hundred of the brothers and sisters at the same time, most of whom are still living, though some have fallen asleep. **First Corinthians 15:6**

Jesus loved His disciples and knew they were struggling with unbelief that He had risen and was alive. Jesus had spent three years with them and had tried to prepare them and tell them what was going to happen.

They were hearing the WORD daily. Yet we know that even though they had Jesus present with them they still struggled. The storm on the Sea of Galilee happened with Jesus right there in the boat with them and they were still afraid. Now with Jesus' death and burial they were even more afraid,

How could Jesus be alive? He was beaten beyond recognition, nailed to a cross, buried and then sealed in the tomb. They had witnessed all of this. Their senses of sight, smell, and hearing were literally screaming, "Jesus is dead!" There was no way He could be alive. As they were sitting in a room having the pity party of

pity parties our Lord Jesus appears before them. He rebukes them for what? He rebukes them for not believing His testimony and the testimony of all those who had seen Him. Later He appeared to the eleven as they sat at the table; and He rebuked their unbelief and hardness of heart, because they did not believe those who had seen Him after He had risen. **Mark 16:14**

31/ GOD IS BIASED TOWARDS US

Father God wants us to understand His love for us. For this reason I bow my knees to the Father of our Lord Jesus Christ, from whom the whole family in heaven and earth is named, that He would grant you, according to the riches of His glory, to be strengthened with might through His Spirit in the inner man, that Christ may dwell in your hearts through faith; that you, being rooted and grounded in love, may be able to comprehend with all the saints what is the width and length and depth and height —to know the love of Christ which passes knowledge; that you may be filled with all the fullness of God. Now to Him who is able to do exceedingly abundantly above all that we ask or think, according to the power that works in us. **Ephesians 3:14--20**

As a father concerned about his sons and their families, I was awakened by the Holy Spirit with a word from the Lord at a very early hour in the morning. I could choose to lie there and perhaps go back to sleep or get up and begin to write. Fortunately for me I chose to get up and began to write. There were several thoughts supported by the Word that I jotted down as the Holy Sprit quickened them in me to give to one of my sons and his wife. After thirty minutes or so, I went back to bed and before I closed my eyes I had this thought, "Will they believe these words?" They will say, "Dad, these are good words, but we know you are biased in our favor." At that moment I heard in my spirit these words I believe were directly from Father God, "If you think you are biased, I am

even more so!" Wow! That was overwhelming! I immediately had a fresh understanding of our Father's love for His children.

This is a very simple Word from the Lord for all of us in the family of God. Our Father in Heaven is biased in His love and thoughts toward each one of us!! Just think about it! Meditate on it! Yes, He loves us so much that He gave us His very Son, our Lord and Savior Jesus Christ! He is biased!

$\mathcal{32}$ OUR FATHER GOD'S COVENANT

So you shall serve the Lord your God, and He will bless your bread and your water. And I will take sickness away from the midst of you.
Exodus 23:25

Father God, our Father, never, that's right never, broke His covenant with His children! Rather His children, the children of Israel, willingly turned their backs on God. The law, which requires justice, was impossible apart from God for man to live by. What the blood of lambs and goats could not do the Blood of the LAMB OF GOD could, did, and is doing in you and in me. Yes, when there was no way, Father God gave His only Son, our Lord Jesus Christ, who freely gave His life that we might live now and forever with HIM!

Jesus, the Bible tells us, has taken His Blood and entered the HOLY OF HOLIES and presented His Blood to seal the New Covenant. The old covenant under the law was good but the New Covenant is even better. Instead of receiving justice I now receive GRACE, all of God's Riches At Christ's Expense. It is grace, grace, God's grace, matchless grace, amazing grace, grace that pardons and cleanses all my sins, grace that heals all my sicknesses and diseases. Yes, it is grace that never, never ends.

Jesus said, "Blessed are the poor in spirit for such is the Kingdom of God." I used to ask for justice. Father God opened my eyes and now I see! I am beggarly poor and in need of Father God's matchless grace. My righteousness is as filthy rags. I traded that for this *beautiful robe of righteousness* **purchased by my Lord and Savior Jesus with His very own BLOOD! It fits perfectly! My sins are gone!**

Let us rejoice and give Him praise. Our God has broken the curse! He lives! We live! How can we not speak and declare His Lordship! He is my Lord and Lord of ALL!

Jesus has spoken, "I HAVE COME THAT YOU WOULD HAVE LIFE, AND THAT ABUNDANTLY!" How can we not declare what we have experienced and heard?

33 HOLY SPIRIT FRUIT

But the fruit of the Spirit is love, joy, peace, longsuffering, kindness, goodness, faithfulness, gentleness, self-control. Against such there is no law. And those who are Christ's have crucified the flesh with its passions and desires. If we live in the Spirit, let us also walk in the Spirit. **Galatians 5:22--25**

The fruit produced by the Holy Spirit in my life is for the benefit of those around me. I cannot eat from the fruit of my tree but need the fruit from the trees of my brothers and sisters. This is one of the reasons that we are instructed by God not to forsake the assembling of ourselves as Christians. We need each other. We affect each other in so many ways. It is important for me to make certain my tree is healthy and producing the fruit it should. My actions will either favorably or adversely affect others in the Body of Christ. This is also evident in God's instructions relative to communion.

34 SPEAK THE WORD

The Word tells me, "as I think in my heart so am I." The Word also says. "out of the abundance of my heart I speak." I have a choice as to what I speak. Isn't it interesting that my tongue controls for the most part my actions as I go through the day? The book of James explains that my tongue is an unruly member of my body. James tells how difficult it is to control the tongue.

What is more fun for us, to talk or to listen? For many of us to be quiet and be still is hard. It seems there has to be something going on even if it is just noise! I need to get in a quiet place and ask Father God what He has for me today. I need the fresh Bread that He has especially prepared for me for this very day!

He has reminded me today that Jesus was addressed by a man, "Good Teacher." Jesus responded, "Why do you call me good? Only God is good!" What was it that Jesus was asking the man? Jesus was asking him, "Do you really know who I am? Do you actually know that I am God?"

So now to receive the Bread for today Father God wants to confirm to me that He alone is God and He alone is good. Also what comes from my mouth is very important. He tells me that, "the power of life and death is in the tongue."

Then I read this verse and know that it is the morsel of Bread for today. Seek good and not evil, That you may live; So the Lord God of hosts will be with you, As you have spoken. **Amos 5:14**

What I believe as I have spiritually eaten this Bread is that I am to seek Father God because He alone is good! Because I am seeking Him He is with me as I go through this day! He will be with me and work through me as I speak! His Word is near me even in my mouth!

35 BODY OF CHRIST

As we have believed in our hearts and confessed with our mouths that Jesus Christ is Lord we are saved. According to Father God's Word we have become the Body of Christ and Jesus is our Head. As we are the Body of Christ, shouldn't we have all of our parts? If all in our Body are ears or all of us are a nose we are pretty ineffective and pretty much useless, not to mention rather strange and maybe funny to look at and be around.

As the Body of Christ we need all of our parts. I need you and you need me. We need each other. We are placed in the Body and told to seek the gifts of the Spirit. Without the Holy Spirit we are just maybe a glob of fat! Do we want to hear what our Father God is saying to the Church or do we want to only hear what tickles our ears?

We need to ask Him to open the *spiritual ears* He has given us and listen. Discernment is often lacking in the body of believers. We need to receive the gifts and operate in the gifts of the Holy Spirit that our Father has given to us to edify and build us up in the faith. *Lambano* is the Greek word that is used in the NT and is interpreted in the English translation receive. It means to aggressively take.

Our Father God has freely given us these wonderful gifts of the Holy Spirit! Let us seek the Lord and take the gifts and let the Holy Spirit move in us as He desires to move! *So God has appointed and placed in the church [for His own use]: first apostles [chosen by Christ], second prophets [those who foretell the future, those who speak a new message from God to the people], third teachers, then those who work miracles, then those with the gifts of healings, the helpers, the administrators, and speakers in various kinds of [unknown] tongues.* **First Corinthians 12:28**

36 GOD WANTS TO SET US FREE

I was starting to believe a lie. God's Word tells us Satan is the father of lies. Our Father God cannot lie. I was beginning to think that my life was pretty much over.

I went to Africa in 2004. I heard the children sing, "I am walking in a miracle life." I experienced several miracles while there. I returned a different man. I was beginning to see miracles here in the United States. Then I went to Africa again in 2006. When I returned from Africa in February some two weeks later I became very ill.

There were some days that I couldn't get up from the floor. As I read the Bible I began to hear in my spirit God ask me this question, "Why do you want to accept ownership of any illness, sickness or disease?" I was more than a little shocked.

My family had pretty much prided itself in keeping accurate records of all illnesses, surgeries, broken bones, scars and every other misfortune. My 95-year-old mother wrote her second book about all of the things she had suffered through. Another question was, "You have faith for others to be healed, but do you have faith for your own personal healing?"

I went to our family doctor and was referred to an infectious disease doctor. He gave me some special antibiotics. The drugs really didn't help. I struggled with this illness, whatever it was, for about six months. I was beginning to think even more that maybe things were coming to the end for me.

Then as I was reading about Moses, I saw that he waited on the Lord. (I had essentially taken ownership of this sickness.) Moses started his incredible walk with God at eighty and when he died he was in very good physical shape. How could this be?

But those who wait on the LORD Shall renew their strength; They shall mount up with wings like eagles, They shall run and not be weary, They shall walk and not faint. **Isaiah 40:31 And then in Psalms we read.** Who satisfies your mouth with good things, So that your youth is renewed like the eagle's. **Psalm 103:5**

I believe His Word is the good thing He has given me. Proverbs tells me that His Word is health to my flesh and strength to my bones. Then I learned the Greek Word *SOZO* is interpreted as saved. It means to make whole spiritually and physically! SOZO appears more than 100 times in the New Testament. This word must be a word that I need to receive and understand! My Lord Jesus is so patient with me! His mercies are new every morning along with the fresh *manna* He has prepared for me to receive!

YES, I was healed and returned to Africa in 2008 and suffered no ill effects during or after the trip!

Our Lord says, "I AM THE LORD WHO HEALS YOU!" Listen! He is talking to you and me!

37 NATIONAL DAY OF PRAYER

Father God, I need you. My neighborhood, my city, my state, my country and the world needs you. Your Word tells me You have and will provide a way when there seems to be no way. You have told me to "pray and not to faint." You have told me to "ask." You have told me as your child to "humble myself and pray."

I know You hear me and I know you care more than I can imagine. You are not deaf. Your arm has not been shortened. You alone can satisfy the needs from the smallest to the largest and You are mighty to perform all you have promised.

I believe the windows of Heaven are open. You have told me to boldly come into your presence. You have dipped Your scepter to me and bid me to come. I am asking this morning for forgiveness and mercy.

You alone are my hope and my salvation. I need You like I have never needed You before. I am beggarly poor in spirit. I say this because Your Son, Jesus Christ, my Lord and Savior, said, "Blessed are the poor in spirit for such is the Kingdom of God."

What this means to me is that I come to You only through and in Him. I have and am nothing in myself. I want all of His grace and mercy to be seen in me. I am asking for you to spare my family, my friends, my neighbors, my city, my state, my country. You alone can spare and save us. I need You.

Come and fill the emptiness in my life and in our land with the overwhelming freshness of Your presence. Your Kingdom and Your will be done here in earth as it is in Heaven!

I am not without hope because, Father God, my hope is in You! Thank you, Jesus, for making the way for me. I am in Your Presence, Father God, and I have Your PEACE! I am forgiven!

Now as I wait, Father God, You will do what you promised! You will forgive my sins and You will heal our land! This is where it's at, in Your presence! "Say no more. Be still and wait!"

38 MARKS OF DISOBEDIENCE

My grandfather, Fountain Chiles Heaton, talked to me as a young boy about the marks he bore in his body because of his disobedience as a child. Grandpa Heaton was a very strict but kind man. He was a godly man and had a very significant influence on my life. So much so, that there was a time in my life when I even referred to God as the God of my grandfather.

The marks that I saw were on his arms. Grandpa always wore long-sleeved shirts and would rarely be seen in an undershirt that would reveal the full length of his arms. The scars were ugly and they looked like swirls of skin, much like the surface of batter in a mixing bowl. A couple of the swirl-like scars had holes that you could see through. Seeing this as a child I wondered what had caused this.

As I now recall this story that Grandpa told me some of the details are not clear as I would like, but enough so that I can tell them:

The time this incident happened was about 1882. Fount, as he was known, was a young boy about 11 years old. He was told not to attempt to move the wash tub of boiling water from the fire. This was a time when water had to be boiled over an open fire for purposes of cooking and for bathing.

As he related this life-changing incident, he said he lifted the tub of water that had been positioned above the fire. In the process of carrying the tub of scalding water he stumbled and fell headfirst into the tub.

The intense pain that would physically last for weeks was immediate and was seemingly unbearable as he passed in and out of consciousness. It was questionable whether he would survive, and if he did his life, based on the word of the doctors of his day, would be shortened.

I believe they put butter on his wounds as they attempted to relieve the pain. They wrapped his head and face along with his arm in clean muslin. Out of respect for some who might read this sort of thing and have a fainting issue I will limit further descriptions of the extent of his wounds.

After 30 days Grandpa's upper body was pretty much all scabs. I remember most his telling about his face. His face miraculously showed little evidence of his near death experience. He said the scab on his face was like a mask and it came off like a mask. He credited God for his recovery and lack of facial scarring.

The marks on my grandfather's body obviously impacted me. I believe it also impacted his eight children and the other twenty-one grandchildren.

The scarring was permanent on his physical body, and as ugly as these scars were, I believe that my grandfather as a result of this experience was resolute in his heart to live every moment thereafter of his life in obedience. Yes, obedience to God was a must in my grandpa's life. He made certain all of his grandchildren heard and understood this message. Children, obey your parents in the Lord, for this is right. "Honor your father and mother," which is the first commandment with promise: "that it may be well with you and you may live long on the earth. **Ephesians 6:1--3**

39 COMMUNION

The Word tells us that we are the Body of Christ. Our Lord Jesus Christ is our Head. Understanding this, we can see that what I do affects you and what you do affects me. What we all do affects our Lord Jesus Christ and all of us as the Body of Christ. Our health and well being is affected by the way we are living our Christian lives.

In Paul's letter to the Church (body of believers) in Corinthians, He addressed a very serious life and death issue. The issue was they were taking communion in an unworthy manner. Like Ananias and Sapphira, the church in Corinth pretended to be living a godly life while continuing to live in their sin.

For every time you eat this bread and drink this cup, you are announcing the Lord's death until he comes again. So anyone who eats this bread or drinks this cup of the Lord unworthily is guilty of sinning against the body and blood of the Lord. That is why you should examine yourself before eating the bread and drinking the cup. For if you eat the bread or drink the cup without honoring the body. of Christ, you are eating and drinking God's judgment upon yourself. That is why many of you are weak and sick and some have even died. But if we would examine ourselves, we would not be judged by God in this way. Yet when we are judged by the Lord, we are being disciplined so that we will not be condemned along with the world. **First Corinthians 11:26--32 (NLT)**

I need to examine myself with the help of the Holy Spirit to address any sin in my life. Not doing this, if I have any unconfessed sin could bring sickness and death into the Body of Christ. Should we not take the remembrance of our Lord Jesus Christ perhaps a little more seriously?

40 WHY DIDN'T SOMEONE TELL ME

Our friend Lyle was lying in his hospital bed diagnosed with terminal cancer. This is what he said, "Why in all the years that I was in the church didn't someone tell me about Jesus?" Walt and I had gone to visit Lyle after hearing that he was in the hospital. Lyle was in his 40's.

He was a very successful businessman, officer in the church, city councilman, former excellent college basketball player, good husband and father. Walt shared Jesus with Lyle during our visit and Lyle accepted Jesus Christ as his personal Savior and Lord. Prior to that moment had Lyle died he would have gone into eternity lost forever and ever.

Yes, even though most of our churches do not speak this word, Lyle would have been destined to hell! Everyone at Lyle's funeral would have testified as to what a good man Lyle had been. Lyle, in the eyes of everyone who knew him was a very good man, a man who loved his family and community, a man who served, gave his talent and time to all around him.

All in attendance would have said surely this man was in heaven. After all, he was a member in good standing of the prominent church in our community. Lyle, no matter how good he may have thought he was or anyone else thought he was, Lyle was headed for hell! Lyle was changed in an instant! Lyle was made whole, He was saved! Jesus Christ was His Lord and Savior!

That night, as I bent over his bedside to tell him goodnight, Lyle hugged me. Something happened to me at that moment. As Walt and I left the hospital and walked into the parking lot I said, "Walt, I believe I have been hugged by Jesus Himself when Lyle hugged me." I was released and given the freedom to hug after that experience. Lyle was now an evangelist. Everyone who came to his bedside heard the message of salvation and they were asked to join hands and pray.

More people were led to Christ and salvation in the few short weeks of Lyle's remaining days here on earth than many others of us would lead in a lifetime. On one of the last days before Lyle went *HOME,* Walt bent over Lyle's bedside. Lyle was now basically blind. Tears from Walt fell on Lyle and Lyle spoke, "Oh, Walt, why are you crying? I am going home to be with Jesus." A few hours later the angels came and took Lyle to heaven! And we know that all things work together for good to them that love God, to them who are the called according to his purpose. **Romans 8:28 (KJV)**

41 WEIGHT OF EVERY SIN (I)

Today as I began my walk I was asking Father God about what I should write. Moments later I noticed, lying at the curb, as I crossed the street a small tire weight that had been lost from a wheel. The weight was only a few ounces. Insignificant? In any race any weight that can be eliminated is a benefit. Any sin no matter how small or insignificant we may think it to be is SIGNIFICANT.

These little weights (sins) that we may tend to ignore begin to weigh us down and all of a sudden we are weary and we wonder why. As we begin this day let us confess to our Father God and ask Him to search our hearts and to cleanse us. Take the "spiritual shower" every morning as we begin our day. Be cleansed and made whole. Then run the day (race) free from every "weight of sin." We are then cleansed from every sin and made whole! We will run today like we have never run before in record time! Can you hear the crowd cheering? You are winning! Our Lord Jesus Christ has given us the victory!

Therefore we also, since we are surrounded by so great a cloud of witnesses, let us lay aside every weight, and the sin which so easily ensnares us, and let us run with endurance the race that is set before us. **Hebrews 12:1**

42 WEIGHT OF EVERY SIN (II)

Previously I wrote about the "WEIGHT OF EVERY SIN." I had asked Father God as I began my walk that day about what He wanted me to write. Moments later I found the tire weight. I wondered at the moment, but by faith I picked it up, and The Holy Spirit who lives in us began to speak to me about this little two-ounce weight. These little weights (sins) initially seem insignificant, but as we run the race we are called to run they can affect our ability to run. And so I wrote.

I also was questioning in my mind whether I should continue to write. Our Father in Heaven and the Holy Spirit living in us knows our every thought and He cares. He will answer every question we have if we will wait and listen. How He answers often will be amazing to us. We are all a part of the Body of Christ. Everything that happens to me affects you and everything that happens to you affects me. This is crazy to the world but to you and me who are being saved it is the power of God! Little did I realize that Pastor David Dodd would read the post that I was led to share about the little weight. More than 2000 miles away, a few days after I had picked up the little weight, David was led by the Holy Spirit to walk to the five-mile point on his walk. Spiritually this is significant. FIVE is the number of power and Divine grace. What did he see lying in the dirt but a second little weight!

Last evening by faith Pastor David placed this second weight in my hand. If Pastor David wasn't listening He would have never picked the little weight up and who would know. My answer from our Father in Heaven was yes, "I want you to continue to write what you hear Me speak. Also to all who read there is a release of healing power and strength and my divine grace I am freely giving to all who will receive!" Our Father God is so good and worthy to receive all of our praise and worship! He alone is God! He tells me in Romans 10, "My Word is near you even in your mouth." Father God wants us to encourage one another with His Words! Speak words of life today to all those around you.

43 LOVE OF GOD

Are not two sparrows sold for a copper coin? And not one of them falls to the ground apart from your Father's will. **Matt 10:29**

That Christ may dwell in your hearts through faith; that you, being rooted and grounded in love, may be able to comprehend with all the saints what is the width and length and depth and height —to know the love of Christ which passes knowledge; that you may be filled with all the fullness of God. **Ephesians 3:17--19**

When you ask or seek to know the dimensions of our Father God's love, you may be surprised to learn what some of the pieces to that question are or the path that God may take you down to gain more understanding.

I have always loved animals. I have hunted and trapped animals. I have butchered them on the farm. I have put down animals that have been injured and unable to recover. I say this to give you some contrast as to what I am about to share.

I have also rescued animals wild and domestic. I have also had many pets. From the time I was around ten years old I was always struck by the Word of God that said "a sparrow does not fall to the ground apart from your Father's will."

It is absolutely amazing that Creator God loves and cares for His creation. The Word also tells us that all of creation groans for His deliverance from the curse of sin. I believe the birds chirping

and singing their songs in the morning and evening are actually songs of praise.

Now for the strange story I believe has given me some better insight into the dimensions of the love of our Father God. On Sunday, July 28, 2013, we heard a faint chirping sound coming from our fireplace wood stove. In the past I have removed swallows that have fallen into the stove and released them to the outdoors. This time when I opened the door there was a baby swallow that was not fully feathered and was trapped and frantically chirping in the damper of the stove. I carefully removed the little creature and was checked when I initially thought of humanely dispatching the helpless little creature.

Instead I got a little box and a piece of my old shirt and placed it along with the helpless little bird now quiet in the shelter of the box.

I found a new syringe and got some non-chlorinated water and carefully gave a drop or two to the little bird. It seemed to be satisfied. So I hunted for and found some earthworms that I smashed and mixed with the water. Then I filled the syringe with this mixture and every couple of hours until dark I would try to give this to the little bird.

It would grasp my finger and perch there while I attempted the feeding process. I struggled with what I was doing. Would it not be better to have just quickly dispatched this little creature? Then I had this thought: God knew that little bird was going to be trapped and He knew I would find it and rescue it as best I could. The Holy Spirit of God emphasized to me the breath of every living creature has come from Him. He is the one who gives and He is the one who takes away.

My brief job was to care for this little creature. I was painting our house on Monday and Tuesday but would take a break every couple of hours to care for the tiny little bird. The first thirty hours it actually seemed to be no worse for wear and then it was obvious that it was weakening. The little bird lived a little over 48 hours. I buried it in our yard and as I did so realized in a new way the incredibly intense love our Father God has for each of us and His little creatures. Every breath we breathe is a gift from God. I actually briefly wept over this little bird and now realized its mission to help me understand in part and in new way the dimensions of our Father God's love. Oh my, how our Father God cares for You and me!!

44 WAIT AND HOPE IN GOD

The world around us is in chaos. It is so easy to get caught up in the turmoil. We all have thoughts and opinions as to what should or should not be done. It is so easy to begin to express our views of things and be figuratively, if not literally, carried away with our rants. When I do this, I find I have allowed my tongue to take control. We are all in various stages of transformation. But this we know, He who has begun a good work in us will complete that work and it will be good.

It is so hard to be still and listen. We need to get away from the noise. We need to silence our cell phones, shut our eyes and listen for at least a few minutes. In this moment of waiting quietly we can hear the clear message of hope and peace that our Heavenly Father has never stopped speaking. He tells me I am His and He has given me a spirit of power, love, and a sound mind. In fact, He tells me He has given me the mind of His Son, my Lord Jesus Christ. He tells me to not be afraid. His peace, the peace of God, will keep my heart and my mind through Christ Jesus. Fear is not from God. He tells me I will stand and be strong in Him. He has given me His Word. By His Word all things exist. Every breath I take is established by His Word! How can I not trust Him?

Through the Lord's mercies we are not consumed, Because His compassions fail not. They are new every morning; Great is Your faithfulness. The Lord is my portion," says my soul, "Therefore I hope in Him!" The Lord is good to those who wait for Him, To the soul who seeks Him. It is good that one should hope and wait quietly For the salvation of the Lord. **Lamentations 3:22--26**

45 SPIRITUAL EYES OF THE CHURCH

Where are the spiritual eyes of the church? Habakkuk tells the watchmen to write down the vision they see. Do we really want to hear what our Father God is saying to us as a people and as a nation? The earthquake in Nepal, the four blood moons, what is happening in the Middle East, the corruption in our government--as these things happen we tend to "bury our heads in the sand." The Enemy wants us to take on the attitude of hopelessness. The Word from our Father in Heaven tells us, "When you see these things, look up for your redemption is drawing near!" Let us wake up and see!

Our Father God has given us the gift of prophecy. The prophets are the spiritual eyes of the Body. We have Hope and a future! Our Hope is our Lord Jesus Christ! "In Him we live and move and have our being!" Let us run to Him! His arms are open wide! There is room for all of us and those around us! Share the Hope that is in you with those around you.

The LORD has brought over you a deep sleep: He has sealed your eyes (the prophets); he has covered your heads (the seers). **Isaiah 29:10 (NIV)**

Behold how pleasant it is for brethren to dwell together in unity! It is like the precious oil upon the head running down on the beard of Aaron, running down on the edge of the garments, It is like the dew of Hermon descending upon the mountains of Zion; for there the Lord commanded the blessing - Life for evermore. **Psalm 133:1--3**

Reuel Theophilus

46 RIGHTEOUSNESS

The Bible tells me all my righteousness is as filthy rags. I am learning what this means. I have held onto what I thought was good and let go of what I thought was bad. After all isn't bad, bad, and good, good? Paul tells us in Romans twelve to be transformed by the renewing of our minds. Then in Corinthians three He tells us we have the mind of Christ. Understanding this, then I can ask Father God to understand and see what needs to change. I see that my goodness that I thought was good is really selfish. Why? Because I LEARN THAT ONLY GOD IS GOOD and that every good and perfect gift comes from Him!

He has given me His goodness and His righteousness through His Son, my Savior, Jesus Christ Why then would I not give up my selfish goodness in order to receive this wonderful gift of righteousness? Father God, help me to receive, aggressively take and not be passive, this wonderful gift of your righteousness, surrender all my selfish goodness for Your perfect robe of righteousness! This righteousness is given through faith in Jesus Christ to all who believe. **Romans 3:22**

47 TRUST

Oh taste and see that the Lord is good. Blessed is the man who trusts in Him. **Psalm 34:8 Children trust those around them before they are five years old. Then they begin to have some doubt and questions. By the time they are ten they have pretty much learned to trust no one. Jesus said, "Anyone who misleads these little ones it would be better to put a millstone around their neck and throw them in the sea." This is one of the reasons I believe it is so important to reach children with the Good News of Jesus. Jesus said, "Suffer the little children to come unto me and forbid them not for such is the Kingdom of God."**

Many of us have trouble trusting because of what we have experienced as a child. We need to come to our Heavenly Father as a child with complete trust in Him. Let us come to Him today trusting and believing every Word He has spoken! What our Father has spoken and speaks He will do. He tells us, "Do not fear. I will save you. I will heal you. Cast all your cares upon Me. All of my promises are yes and amen in Christ Jesus." Having put our trust in Him we will not be disappointed! Yes, taste and see OUR LORD IS GOOD!!

48 THE LITTLE CHURCH

In 2004 I had the privilege to go to Tanzania, East Africa. Standing in a field adjacent to the little church that had been built there in the jungle, I heard in my spirit these words, "What you see before you is also in Auburn, Washington. If you will take care of the little church I will take of the big church."

At that moment, what I physically saw in the distance, as I looked across a vast field of maize stubble dotted with large ant castles, was the roof and spire of a very large church building. This was a large edifice and had little involvement with the people there in jungle.

Our Father God is so patient with me. He knows everything about me. Six years later, as I had begun to regularly ride a two-mile circle through the neighborhood where we lived. I began to understand what my LITTLE CHURCH was. It was exactly where I lived, The LITTLE CHURCH was my neighborhood. I began to pray as I rode and began to meet my neighbors.

At first, I prayed very generally, I began to meet some and to learn names. I had some very interesting learning experiences. Listening and not talking too much was really hard for me. Praying specifically for individual needs of those in the neighborhood as they agreed to be prayed for was a very wonderful experience for me. I have much to learn.

I believe, with God's help, as one person, we can make a difference where we live.

49 WORD FROM THE CROSS

After thirty-three years, with the last three in ministry our Lord Jesus willingly gives His life and allows Himself to be crucified on a cross. Our Lord Jesus, beaten beyond recognition and now hanging naked and exposed from the cross speaks,

(To the leaders and people)"Father forgive them for they know not what they do."

(To the thief) "This day you shall be with Me in paradise."

(To Mary & John) "Woman, behold your son. Behold your mother."

(To Father God) "My God, My God, why have You forsaken Me?"

"I thirst."

"It is finished."

(To Father God) "Father, into Your hands I commend My spirit."

With these final words, our Lord Jesus completed the salvation plan that He and Father God made before all creation with one incredible finale to come. In three days the resurrection of our Lord Jesus Christ would defeat the last remaining curse of sin! Death itself would lose all its power! Amazing love! Amazing grace! The shed Blood of Jesus cleanses us and we have been set free! All other religions and their prophets remain in their graves.

Our Lord Jesus Christ is alive! He has risen! He ever lives to make intercession for us that where He is we may be also! Let the redeemed of the Lord say so! Our Lord has risen! He lives! Praise the Lord! We live and move and have our being in Him!

50 PHARISEE

What would you think about a person who had memorized five books of the Bible, prayed six hours a day and fasted two days every week? Do you think they would make a good elder or deacon in your church?

Jesus dealt with a whole group of very religious people like this. They were known as Pharisees. They were deaf and blind spiritually. They wanted justice. Their justice insisted that Jewish converts to Christianity should be stoned. A man named Saul was complicit in the stoning of Stephen. Saul was a Pharisee of Pharisees and was very justice minded.

I personally used to ask for justice. I didn't understand the Beatitude that Jesus spoke when He said, "Blessed are the poor in spirit for such is the Kingdom of God." When I came to understand what this verse meant I realized that I am beggarly poor and need all of Father God's mercy and grace! I now pray and ask for mercy! It is good to pass from death to life, to surrender and accept the Lord Jesus as Savior and Lord and to begin the path of understanding and be led by the Holy Spirit!

5/ WAIT ON THE LORD

What about wait don't we understand? No one in our culture wants to wait. The world around us says why should you wait when you can have it now? After all, you deserve it! It is your right! For me to wait means that I understand. I get it. My Father in Heaven is telling me to wait. By waiting I am being obedient. My Father tells me my obedience is better than my sacrifices. By waiting I am acknowledging Him as Lord and sovereign God. My act of waiting demonstrates to Him that I believe Him. As I wait He will do what He has promised.

He has told me that ALL of His promises are yes and amen in Christ Jesus. He has promised me that as I wait He will provide all my needs, make me whole, renew my strength and give me His peace and joy. The Creator of the universe, Father God, who spared not His own Son for me, says, "WAIT." Why would I not wait? It would seem to be so obvious. Do you suppose I am spiritually blind and deaf if not stubborn and self-willed? Father, forgive me! I was blind but now I see!

52 CAST YOUR CARE ON FATHER GOD

Why do we struggle when we are offered the very best? We are so independent and at the end of the day we are exhausted and we wonder why! Father God wants us to come to Him! We take pride in saying I did this myself. So much so that we can often miss the incredible offer that our Father God, the Creator of the universe is offering.

He is saying, "Look, I made you and I know exactly what you need. First of all you need ME. Secondly, you need each other. Oh by the way give ME your cares!" When I humble myself and say, "Father God, I need You." My world immediately begins to get better. It continues to get better then as I show myself to be friendly to those around me.

God's Word says that if I want friends I need to show myself to be friendly. Then the icing on this good thing that is now in process is that I can give my cares to Father God and I can trust and be at peace knowing He will bring me through! This through is not just getting by or just barely making it! It is a victorious through! He gives victory when we do this!

We are now in position to be more than conquerors because our Father God gives all of His resources to give us success! We win together with God and each other!

Acknowledge Father God and He is right there with us to direct our steps! Likewise you younger people, submit yourselves to your elders. Yes, all of you be submissive to one another, and be clothed with humility, for "God resists the proud, But gives grace to the humble. Therefore humble yourselves under the mighty hand of God, that He may exalt you in due time, casting all your care upon Him, for He cares for you. **First Peter 5:5--7**

53 EYE GATE

In today's world we must decide in advance that we are going to guard the gates or entry to our hearts. Our Father God's Word tells us that, "as we think in our hearts so are we." Pictures or videos are now available not only in books or magazines but readily available in the wireless devices that are now held in our hands. These devices are not evil. Like everything in our lives we must choose how we will use them.

What will we allow ourselves to look at? Our Father God has given us a new heart, His heart! We are transformed by the renewing of our minds through His Word to us. Like Joshua I must choose whom I will serve. My Father God wants me to be holy even as He is holy. I want my eyes to be His eyes. I will shut my eyes if I have to. I only want to see what is good. I have confessed my sin. The Blood of Jesus, my Savior and Lord, cleanses me from all unrighteousness. The Holy Spirit is helping me to guard my eye gate! Let us choose this day not to live like and look like the world around us! I am, we are God's kids!

54 ENOCH

In the Book of Revelation we learn that we overcome the Enemy by the Blood of the Lamb and the word of our testimony. We learn the testimony of Enoch when we read in Genesis and Hebrews that Enoch pleased God. How did He please God? He believed God! He had faith and believed the Word of God. He walked with God for 365 years before God took Him. He didn't die! He was a God Pleaser! He believed! I want to be a God Pleaser! Enoch walked with God; and he was not, for God took him. **Genesis 5:24**

Enoch was taken away so that he did not see death, and was not found, because God had taken him; for before he was taken he had this testimony, that he pleased God. But without faith it is impossible to please Him, for he who comes to God must believe that He is, and that He is a rewarder of those who diligently seek Him. **Hebrews 11:5--6**

55 CHANGE

Just mention the word change and you can almost feel the tension build. Most people want to be comfortable. They don't want to change. They like for the most part to be where they are.

However, in our world change is all around us. Things are changing daily. Some changes are better than others. Some changes are easier to accept than others. As we think about it, probably we can all agree that we are living in a world of change.

With all of the change then and our dissatisfaction with change, something or someone that is changeless should be a welcome relief to us. I would suggest the Word of God and Father God Himself is that welcome relief. I need the stability of God Himself in me through His Holy Spirit presence and His daily Word to me to even come close to making it in the world we now live in.

Yes, Lord Jesus, I choose to serve You in this rapidly and continuously changing world we are living in. Without You I can't make it! I believe and know You will bring me safely through!

56 JESUS WEPT

Therefore when Jesus saw her weeping, and the Jews who came with her weeping, He groaned in the spirit and was troubled. **John 11:1** And He said, "Where have you laid him?" They said to Him, "Lord, come and see." Jesus wept. Then the Jews said, "See how He loved him!" And some of them said, "Could not this Man, who opened the eyes of the blind, also have kept this man from dying?" Then Jesus, again groaning in Himself, came to the tomb. **John 11:34--38**

I believe my Lord Jesus groaned, wept and groaned again because those He dearly loved didn't believe. I pray, Lord, for forgiveness for my unbelief. Faith is a gift from You and I ask for and believe I am receiving the gift of faith. I know You are at the right hand of Father God right now interceding for me and my brothers and sisters this very moment!

I believe Your Word to me that You give me. Help me to encourage and share the "Daily Bread" that You are giving to me. It is Your Word not mine. Your Word is truth and life. I pray that You will take joy in our belief and we will be one in You and You in us as we walk together and share according to Your Word You are giving daily to us. Be glorified in Your Temple! Lord Jesus, we are Your Temple! Lord Jesus, we are Your Body and You are our Head!

And they heard the sound of the Lord God walking in the garden in the cool of the day, and Adam and his wife hid themselves from the presence of the Lord God among the trees of the garden. Then the Lord God called to Adam and said to him, "Where are you? **Genesis 3:8--9**

Our Lord God is calling to us as He walks. He calls, "Where are you? I am here," He says, "Why are you hiding from me?" Having received His Son, our Lord Jesus Christ, our relationship with the Father has been restored!

He wants us to come to Him boldly and seek His face. Can you get a hold on this, that Creator God desires relationship daily, hourly and yes, moment by moment with each one of us? He wants a relationship that includes Him in all we do! Let's answer His call and say, "Here I am. I am running to You, Father God. Your Son, my Savior, has made the way back to you and I am running straight to You!"

57 A WORD

Many of us today are going here and there seeking a Word from the Lord. Why not go directly to our Lord Jesus for that Word? Our Lord Jesus is the Word and continues to say, "Come unto Me!" Yes, He is saying, "Come. Open my Word and you will hear what I have to say to you."

I believe if you will take your Bible and open it to the Book of Proverbs the very first chapter you will hear a Word from our Lord Jesus specifically for you. I could copy Proverbs 1 for you right here in this devotion, but I believe our Father in Heaven wants you to see and hear and then know by faith He has spoken directly to you.

As You do this by faith, I am asking the Holy Spirit to emphasize to you a Word from Him that is personal to you. If you don't hear it in the first chapter, read the second chapter, and, if necessary, the third. Remember as you read you are eating and drinking the Living Word of God! And you have responded to His Word, "COME unto Me!" Father God wants you to know that in your obedience to His Word you are blessed!

Here is the Word that the Holy Spirit confirmed to me from Proverbs one through three that I just read moments ago. Listen! Listen! Listen! He continues to speak in these three Proverbs and He is saying, "Listen to Me! I am Creator God and as you read and listen you will receive understanding!" Trust in the Lord. He is your security. His Word is health to your flesh and strength to your bones. **Proverbs 3:8.**

58 PRAY FOR MERCY

My heart is broken as we continue to ignore what is happening. I pray and ask for mercy! Many around us call themselves Christians and say what the Bible says doesn't matter! We have bent over backwards not to offend anyone. The truth is that our Bible tells us that not everyone is going to Heaven. The word Hell is rarely heard coming from our pulpits today.

I don't want anyone to go to Hell and my Bible tells me that my Father in Heaven doesn't want anyone to go to Hell. However, my Bible clearly says there is a Heaven and a Hell. My Bible exudes the love of God and tells us of His provision by giving His Son, our Lord Jesus, to save us and make a way for us to live eternally and be with Him. Without our Lord Jesus Christ the world and this nation are lost. Many of our friends and neighbors are lost and destined to Hell. Do I care? My Father God does and He wants me to believe Him and share the hope I have. That hope is Jesus Christ!

Father God clearly says that if my people who are called by My Name, that's those of us who claim the Name of Jesus, will humble ourselves and pray and ask for forgiveness, He will hear us and forgive us and heal our land.

Father God, I believe Your Word. You alone are God. I am sorry. You are my only hope. Forgive me. I plead for mercy and ask for Your help to honor my Lord Jesus Christ in all that I do. Shine, Jesus, Shine! You are my HOPE! All around is sinking sand but on the SOLID ROCK I STAND!

59 PEACE IN THE STORM

Often we wait until we are in the middle of the storm to seek help. Even then many of us go everywhere but to the Lord. We do this over and over again and expect a different outcome. Why do we continue to be so stubborn? Our Father continues to speak to us and calls us, "Come." It is so simple we have difficulty believing and accepting His invitation.

The best course of action is to fix our mind on Him before the storm. But if we have waited and not done that and we are now in the storm, because He is so merciful His arms are still open. We should not hesitate but run! Yes, run to Him now!

Thou wilt keep him in perfect peace, whose mind is stayed on thee: because he trusteth in thee. **Isaiah 26:3 (KJV)**

60 TODAY'S BREAD

Today when I asked for fresh Bread this is what I received. "Would you like to have fellowship with Jesus? Open your Bible and start to read. He is the Word!"

Wow!! So I did. Then this verse came to mind. Behold I stand at the door and knock. If any man hear my voice and open the door I will come into Him and sup and He with me. **Revelation 3:20**

I need fresh Bread every day. Sometimes I need more Bread. There is always enough to meet my need. I can have as much as I want and it is always fresh. Our Lord Jesus is that Bread! He will always satisfy my every need! He is saying, "Take. Eat."

So they gathered it every morning, every man according to his need. **Exodus 16:21**

61 IDENTITY

One of the first things that happens as Christians is our identity is attacked. Our enemy (Satan himself) does not want us to know who we are. He will attack our identity. **I am everything my Father God says I am.**

The people around us are not our enemy. If those around us do not guard their tongues they can be used by the enemy to attack or challenge our identity. We all need to guard our tongues and choose to always speak life. When our identity is challenged, it is important to understand that we are God's child, His son or daughter. As His child, we are not insignificant. We matter. We have been given authority and power through our Lord Jesus Christ!

Father God, help me to understand who I am and to walk in the authority and power You have given me. Behold! I have given you authority and power to trample upon serpents and scorpions, and [physical and mental strength and ability] over all the power that the enemy [possesses]; and nothing shall in any way harm you. **Luke 10:19**

For ye are all sons of God, through faith, in Christ Jesus. **Galatians 3:26 (ASV)**

62 PRESENCE OF THE LORD

There are days when you may not feel the presence of the Lord. Is our Father God any less present? The good news is our Heavenly Father is always present. His presence is not limited to our feelings! He is present in all of His fullness and glory! Praise the Lord! Even when we feel we are at our lowest point!

His presence is based on His Word. He is changeless. His Son, our Lord Jesus Christ, ever lives to intercede for us. Lo, I am with you always even unto the end of the age. **Matt 28:20**

Our part then is to believe His Word. His Word tells us that we must believe that He is and that he is the Rewarder of those that diligently seek Him. Our walk is a faith walk, not a feeling walk.

Reuel Theophilus

63 FEAR NOT

In our world almost everything that is not from God is promoted by fear. How do we know that it is not from God? We know because God's Word tells us that He has not given us a spirit of fear. If we do not know what our Heavenly Father has spoken, we can get caught up in the hysteria. Our Lord Jesus Christ is our anchor. He is the Solid Rock. His Word is life! His Word is truth. His Word never changes. He has given His Word that He is in control of what happens in the earth, on the earth and to the earth. He created the earth. All things were made by Him!

If we don't know the Word we are going to be tossed to and fro and pulled here and there and still be insecure. The issue of **GLOBAL WARMING IS IN GOD'S HANDS!**

While the earth remains, Seedtime and harvest, Cold and heat, Winter and summer, And day and night Shall not cease. **Genesis 8:22**

64 BELIEVE GOD'S WORD

All things are possible with our Father God. Nothing, that's right, nothing is too difficult for Him. He wants me to ask. He tells us to ask. Jesus would ask, "What do you want me to do for you?" If we don't ask we really can't expect to receive anything. When we ask we are obedient. When we ask His Word tells us that, "we must believe that He is and the rewarder of those who diligently seek Him."

Abraham believed as we learn in Genesis fifteen and what happened? He received. Father God, I pray You will help me today. You are my refuge and strength. You have told me to COME, ASK, and RECEIVE. Here I am, Lord. I have brought my need to You. I am waiting. I will wait. Because I know you, I know I will receive!

And he believed in the Lord, and He accounted it to him for righteousness. **Genesis 15:6**

65 VOICE OF GOD

Our Father in Heaven is speaking. Who is He talking to? Samuel as a young boy initially didn't realize that God was speaking to Him. All I have to do is open my Bible and say, "Father God, I need to hear from You." Immediately I know He has been waiting because He has extended the invitation again and again to come to Him.

Immediately as I begin to read I have peace, peace that passes all understanding! Why did I wait? In His presence I have peace and I am secure. The very best is mine because every good and perfect gift comes from Him and His heart is to bless me. He has told me that His good thoughts towards me are more numerous than the sands of the sea.

But whoever listens to me will dwell safely, And will be secure, without fear of evil. **Proverbs 1:33**

66 OVERCOMING THE DEVIL

We overcome the enemy by the Blood of the Lamb and the word of our testimony. I continually remind myself that people are not the enemy. People allow themselves to be used by the enemy but they are not the enemy. Satan himself is the enemy. He has come to steal, kill and destroy.

Our battlefield is our mind. We are instructed in Romans 12:2 to be transformed by the renewing of our minds. The Word in our minds and hearts changes us. Sometime ago I was struggling with depressive thinking and then I read in Nehemiah 8:10 these words, *"The joy of the Lord is your strength."* Those eight words in an instant changed everything for me! Man shall not live by bread alone but every Word that comes from the mouth of God. Jesus said, "Take, eat, this is my Body broken for you!" The Word from our Heavenly Father will change everything for us! It is Life! The joy of the Lord is your strength!

67 WAIT, WAIT, WAIT

WAIT, Wait, wait, no matter how you write it or say it no one today likes to wait or wants to wait! Why should you wait when you can have it now? Instant gratification is demanded and people are very troubled when there is any delay or they are required to wait.

However, when I listen to what my heavenly Father is speaking to me I often hear the Word, "WAIT." Wait on the LORD: be of good courage, and he shall strengthen thine heart: wait, I say, on the LORD. **Psalm 27:14**

Rest in the Lord, and wait patiently for Him; Do not fret because of him who prospers in his way, Because of the man who brings wicked schemes to pass. Cease from anger, and forsake wrath; Do not fret—it only causes harm. For evildoers shall be cut off; But those who wait on the Lord, They shall inherit the earth. **Psalm 37:7--9**

But those who wait on the Lord Shall renew their strength; They shall mount up with wings like eagles, They shall run and not be weary, They shall walk and not faint. **Isaiah 40:31**

68 GOD AND TIME

But, beloved, do not forget this one thing, that with the Lord one day is as a thousand years, and a thousand years as one day. **Second Peter 3:8 Time is not an issue with our Father God. Thinking about second Peter 3:8 for a moment challenges our minds. From God's perspective, Jesus ascended into Heaven two days ago. Methuselah almost lived a day. The United States has only been a country for five hours and forty-nine minutes. A person who lives to be one hundred by our calendar would only have lived two hours and twenty-four minutes according to second Peter 3:8. Continuing this thought, the average person lives about an hour.**

Little wonder then, we read in James that our life is a brief vapor. whereas you do not know what will happen tomorrow. For what is your life? It is even a vapor that appears for a little time and then vanishes away. **James 4:14**

Apart from our Lord Jesus Christ and our Father God we are truly nothing. How can any of us think we can delay choosing who we will serve? Our Lord Jesus continues to say, "Come unto me, COME, yes, COME unto me!" Run with me to HIM!

69 KNOWLEDGE VS. KNOWING

Knowing about God is good but vastly different from knowing God. Knowing God comes through a personal relationship with Him. Through my personal relationship with Him I learn His faithfulness to me. The more I trust Him the better my life becomes.

From the knowledge side, I read that He has a plan for my life. From a relationship side, I know He has a good plan for me. From a relationship side, I want to not just know about the plan but I want to live in God's plan for my life. Through Jesus when He prayed in John seventeen we learn that, "it is eternal life to know Him and Jesus Christ whom He sent." It is overwhelming to know the daily garden experience that Adam and Eve had with Father God has been restored! The garden is our heart and we can commune with Him anytime anywhere!

Trust in the Lord with all your heart, And lean not on your own understanding; In all your ways acknowledge Him, And He shall direct your paths. **Proverbs 3:5--6**

70 WORDS OF LIFE

As a people we go everywhere seeking something that will satisfy. We want to be entertained. We desire entertainment! In America millions fill our stadiums while our churches struggle to keep the doors open. Our sports teams have become our "sacred cows." Happiness depends to a large extent on whether our team has won!

With the world around us in such a mess people are seeking anything that will allow them to escape the reality of the real world. We Christians have the answer. The answer is Jesus Christ our Lord crucified, risen and soon-coming King! We are so afraid we will offend someone that we water down the gospel, live like the world and hope for the best. No matter what happens it seems the most important thing we are trying to do is make sure everyone is having fun!

The reality is the fun is only momentary! People all around us are not having fun. There are suicides, children born outside of marriage, abortions, divorces, many sick and even dying, and many of these are Christians. How will they hear without a life lived before them that is different? Let us live a life that demonstrates Christ's love! Let us live a life that believes, speaks and lives the WORDS OF LIFE spoken by our Lord Jesus Christ! There is forgiveness and cleansing. Repentance is a word no one seems to want to hear. Please, let us repent and return to our God. He alone can save us!

Let us come out from among them and let us live today as ambassadors for our Lord Jesus walking in the power and authority He has given us. Jesus said, "This is the way. Walk in it!" We are God's kids. Let us live like whose we are!

71 GOD'S PROMISES

God's promises are for you and for me. Our God is no respecter of persons. He loves and cares for each of us more than we can understand or comprehend. God's promises are certain. Our responsibility is twofold.

First, Father God wants me to believe His Word to me. Secondly, I believe Father God wants me to wait on Him. As I wait He doesn't want me to try and help myself out by substituting something that is not from Him to help Him out. Once I have His promise, I believe and wait and as I wait I give Him praise for the fulfillment of His promise I am about to receive. How do I know? Because His Word says, All of the promises of God are yes and amen in Christ Jesus. Second Corinthians 1:20

Father God's answer is, "Yes! Yes, I will meet your need! Yes, I will save that loved one! Yes, I have a job for you! Yes, I will bring you safely through! Yes! Yes! Yes!" Please listen, I believe you can hear Him! He is saying, "I hear! I care! I will meet your need!"

Reuel Theophilus

72 GOD IN A BOX

In my walk with God I have often found that I have tried to put our Heavenly Father God in a box. This happens when I think the revelation I have come to understand is the way God is. Yes, He may be all of that, but in reality He is infinite! More than I can imagine! Now we see through a glass darkly. We only know in part. Our Heavenly Father is far bigger than any box any man or group of men might attempt to get our Heavenly Father to fit into. Our Father God is far beyond any of man's known boundaries. Praise the Lord. He alone is God and worthy to receive all glory honor and praise! Let everything that has breath praise the Lord!

73 JESUS INTERCEDES FOR US

There is nothing like hearing our Father God speak and He is speaking. If you have received Jesus Christ as Lord and Savior, Father God wants you to know that our Lord Jesus is at His right hand this very moment interceding for you. Your every need is being presented and petitioned to our Father in Heaven by our Lord Jesus Christ. He will provide that need according to His riches in glory through Christ Jesus!

Now I know that the LORD saves His anointed; He will answer him from His holy heaven With the saving strength of His right hand. Some trust in chariots, and some in horses; But we will remember the name of the LORD our God. **Psalm 20:6--7**

74 BLESSINGS FOR OUR CHILDREN

I really don't know anyone who comes to talk with me who doesn't want their children and their grandchildren blessed. I believe our Bible tells us that when we walk with God as He has called us to walk, this blessing we desire is promised to us by our Father God. Our Lord Jesus tells us He came to fulfill the Law and we fulfill His commandments when we love the Lord our God with all our heart and love our neighbors as we love ourselves.

I don't get to choose whom I love when I walk with God. Father God, help me to love as You have called me to love. You loved me while I was yet a sinner and all messed up. My love doesn't get it. I need your love, the love you describe for me in First Corinthians 13. Your love doesn't get upset and doesn't keep a record of any offense that is experienced. Your love never fails. In Jesus' Name, Amen.

As I do this, Your promise to me is that my children and their children will be blessed! But the mercy of the Lord is from everlasting to everlasting On those who fear Him, And His righteousness to children's children, To such as keep His covenant, And to those who remember His commandments to do them. **Psalm 103:17--18**

75 I AM A FRIEND OF GOD

Father God, Your Word tells me to be transformed by the renewing of my mind. Now considering this, I believe You want me to grab hold of this thought, that You, Creator God, want to be my best Friend. I have knowledge of this but You want me to KNOW the reality of it! YES! Yes, I am the friend of God. What more could I ask? As the Friend of God I have it all! I lack nothing!

Father God, only You can satisfy! Father God, I pray that You will help me, along with all those who are reading this day, to more clearly see and understand the reality of the relationship we have with You! As we see we are transformed! Your WORD is truth and we are set free! Delight yourself also in the Lord, And He shall give you the desires of your heart. **Psalm 37:4**

76 LOVE STORY TESTIMONY

Our Father God took a boy from Indiana and a girl from Pennsylvania and sent them to a Christian college in Illinois. They have a date and Father God talks to them through the Holy Spirit individually after the date and they both know they will marry.

Satan has come to steal, kill and destroy. Father God knew this and knew what Satan was going to try to do to the boy and then would do to the girl. As God's kids, He told the boy this girl was the right choice and told the girl this boy was the right choice. Satan was and is a loser!

Six months later the boy had a nervous breakdown. The doctors told the girl the boy would never get well and she should forget about him. The boy committed himself to a mental hospital in Oregon. After three months in the hospital and numerous electroshock treatments to cause the boy to have amnesia, the doctors told the boy if he wanted to get well not to set foot inside a church again.

Father God healed the boy while he was in the hospital apart from the doctors. Upon the boy's release, he went to work in a factory and took none of the prescribed medications. The girl came that summer to see the boy in Oregon. The boy asked the girl to marry him and she told the boy she wanted to finish her college training. The boy then told her he would join the army while he waited for her.

He joined the army and the army talked to the boy's doctor in Salem, Oregon. The doctor was delighted. In the army the boy would not be seeking God and in the doctor's mind, he had won. The boy would not be in church. He told the army doctor who called him the boy would be a good soldier. He was right on that point. The boy was a good soldier, but he didn't understand the boy was also God's soldier.

Six months later the army orders happened to work out so the soldier boy would be able to give the girl an engagement ring in her family home in Pennsylvania. Then it would work out a year later they would be married just as Father God had shown them! That was fifty-nine years ago! And we know that all things work together for good to them that love God, to them who are the called according to his purpose. **Romans 8:28 (KJV)**

77 DECIDE

In America today we are still blessed to be able to freely go and come as we choose. What we will have to deal with tomorrow to a large extent will be the result of the decisions and choices we make today.

My first choice needs to be, I will serve the Lord. Every day I need to make that choice, just as Joshua declared, "Choose you this day whom you will serve. As for me and my house we will serve the Lord."

Father God, I choose You this day and I am listening to Your Word. Your Word is telling me to make known Your faithfulness. I will sing of the mercies of the Lord forever; With my mouth will I make known Your faithfulness to all generations. **Psalm 89:1** Let everything that has breath praise the Lord. Praise the Lord. **Psalm 150:6**

78 RELATIONSHIP WITH FATHER GOD

Father God, You want us to know You as Almighty God, as Lord, as Friend, as Comforter, as Healer, as Deliverer, as Provider, as Protector, as Father, as Confidant, as Lawyer. Yes, You want us to know You as our All-in-all.

You want us to worship You in spirit and in truth, worship in song and speech by and through the Word of God which is near us in our hearts and mouths. We are called of God to speak His Words of life in everything we do. Even in our speech, He gives us the words if we are listening. This verse in Exodus I saw for the first time in this way personally last week!

So the LORD said to him, "Who has made man's mouth? Or who makes the mute, the deaf, the seeing, or the blind? Have not I, the LORD? Now therefore, go, and I will be with your mouth and teach you what you shall say." **Exodus 4:11--12**

79 WORSHIP

Father God tells us in His Word we are to worship in spirit and in truth. Jesus makes it clear to us the Word is truth. What this means then is we should sing our praises using the Word of God. David understood this and we see Him doing this in the Psalms. Father God is pleased and we are blessed when we sing His Word in our praise and worship. There is power in the Word and there is power in our songs when we sing the Word of God!

But the hour is coming, and now is, when the true worshipers will worship the Father in spirit and truth; for the Father is seeking such to worship Him. God is Spirit, and those who worship Him must worship in spirit and truth. **John 4:23--34**

80 HELP

When we face a crisis situation, where can we go for help? Our Father God tells us He is our refuge. He wants us to come to Him. Knowing this, the first place we should go is to our Father God.

We need to run to Him! His arms are open and He can and will meet every need! He has unlimited resources! He has promised to supply ALL of our needs according to His riches in glory through Christ Jesus!

Do you need help today? Come, let us run together to our Father God. Tell Him everything! Don't hold back. Help is only a prayer away! His arm has not been shortened and He is not deaf! He will do all He has promised beyond anything we can imagine!! He spared not His own Son while we were yet sinners. How much more will He do for us now that we are His children! God is our refuge and strength, A very present help in trouble. **Psalm 46:1**

81 FAITH TO FACE DIFFICULTIES

Our Father God wants us to walk by faith and not by sight. When the situation becomes difficult and everything seems to be against me, will I be overcome by my circumstances?

My Heavenly Father wants me to have victory! He wants me to believe and trust Him for victory! No matter how difficult what I am facing may be, my Heavenly Father is greater! I have His Word! His Word to me is I will deliver You! I will protect you! I will defend you! I will heal you! Having put my trust in Him I am more than a conqueror!

But without faith it is impossible to please Him, for he who comes to God must believe that He is, and that He is a rewarder of those who diligently seek Him. **Hebrews 11:6**

82 OVERWHELMED

Today there is someone reading this who is feeling overwhelmed. Father God loves you and is saying, "Come all of you who are weak and heavy laden and I will give you rest!" He alone can deliver and save us.

His has given us His Word. He sent us His Word. Be still and listen. You will hear His voice. He is gently speaking, "You are mine! I have you in my hand I will never let you go. Receive and believe my Word to you this day. I am your Healer and Deliverer! My Word will not return void. I will do what I have promised! Receive my Word and let faith replace your feelings! Receive my peace and my joy! My perfect love casts out all fear!" God is our refuge and strength, a very present help in trouble. **Psalm 46:1**

83 COME TO THE FATHER

Father God, Your Word is life! Your Word is the only thing that will satisfy every longing and need I have! Your arms are open wide and You are calling out to me, "COME, Come, yes, come to Me, come!" Father God, You are my refuge and strength! Father God, You are my ever-present help in time of need! I wait no longer. I am running to You! You are my Hope! I put my trust in You! In You, Lord, I am safe and secure! There's room for you, too! There is room for us all! Don't think any longer, just come to the Father. He is waiting for us to come!

It is written in the prophets, And they shall be all taught of God. Every man therefore that hath heard, and hath learned of the Father, cometh unto me. **John 6:45**

$\mathcal{84}$UNLOAD OUR CARES

And Moses spake so unto the children of Israel: but they hearkened not unto Moses for anguish of spirit, and for cruel bondage. **Exodus 6:9**

There are times our cares weigh so heavily it is difficult to receive the Word being spoken to us. Fortunately, we have a loving Father who cares more than we can imagine. He tells us to cast all of our cares upon Him because He cares for us. His Son, our Lord Jesus, tells us a sparrow does not fall to the ground without His consent. That being true, He reminds us we are more valuable than the sparrows. Since He cares for the sparrows, we can be certain He cares for us!

We need to let go of our cares and give them all to Him. I want to receive and walk in His strength so I can receive His Word to me each day. I want to walk in His wonder-working power and authority He wants His children to have and walk in. He wants me to be free of this world's cares! I want to clearly hear and obey His Word to me! I believe and I receive! His Word is near me in my heart and in my mouth! **Deuteronomy 30:14**

85 GOD WILL SUPPLY ALL NEEDS

Father God wants us to understand He wants the best for us. He is a good Father. Jesus said, "If an earthly father has a son who asks for bread will he give him a stone? If an earthly father knows how to give good gifts, how much more will our Heavenly Father do."

The Word our Heavenly Father wants us to hear today is that He cares. He is our ever-present help in time of need. There is no need we have He won't supply. We need to believe His Word and act upon it. We need to ask and believe He will do what He has promised. His Word will not return void.

Beloved, I pray that you may prosper in all things and be in health, just as your soul prospers. **Third John 2**

86 LISTEN UP

When Father God says, "Listen," I know it is something He wants me to hear. He wants me to know I know, that I know. Yes, He wants me to know. He also wants me to share and remind you because you may already know.

Now what is it our Heavenly Father wants us to know? He wants us to know our relationship with Him has been fully restored. He has fully accepted the sacrifice of our Lord Jesus Christ for all of our sins. As evidence of His acceptance of that sacrifice, our Lord Jesus rose from the grave.

Now hear this!! Father God, with the resurrection of our Lord Jesus Christ, has given His witness to our full and complete salvation! When we believe in our heart and confess with our mouth we accept Jesus, His Son, as our Lord and Savior, we become the beneficiaries of His love and grace. Our relationship with Father God through His Son, our Lord Jesus, is now fully restored!

Listen! Listen! Listen! "You, my children, are my friends!"

Did you hear that? You and I are the friends of God!! Henceforth I call you not servants; for the servant knoweth not what his lord doeth: but I have called you friends; for all things that I have heard of my Father I have made known unto you. **John 15:15 (KJV)**

87 WALK BY FAITH NOT BY SIGHT

Thus the Lord saved Israel that day out of the hand of the Egyptians; and Israel saw the Egyptians dead upon the sea shore. And Israel saw that great work which the Lord did upon the Egyptians: and the people feared the Lord, and believed the Lord, and his servant Moses. **Exodus 14:30--31**

The children of Israel in this passage believed God because they saw the miracle of God. In the New Testament Jesus told Thomas he believed because Thomas saw Jesus' wounds. Then Jesus said, "Blessed are those who believe who have not seen." This is you and I. Every time I hear the Word of God, I need to believe. I must not let the way I feel or what I see change what I believe and know to be true. Father God has told us and we believe. Father God says, "My Word will not return void."

Believing, we receive and are blessed beyond anything we can imagine! Father God, help me with this. I am what You say I am. I have what you say I have. I believe You! I believe You! I believe You! Oh my, how I am blessed! My cup is full and running over! More, Lord, more. More of You, more of You!

But without faith it is impossible to please him: for he that cometh to God must believe that he is, and that he is a rewarder of them that diligently seek him. **Hebrews 11:6 (KJV)**

88 TRUST AND OBEY

Our Father God wants the very best for His children. He is biased towards you and me! He will withhold no good thing from us. This being true, why do we struggle? Be still! Listen! You will hear and recognize His still, small voice.

Trust in the Lord with all your heart, And lean not on your own understanding; In all your ways acknowledge Him, And He shall direct your paths. **Proverbs 3:5-6**

Father God, thank you for the rain! Spiritually and physically, Father God, we need You to water us with Your Holy Spirit living water and refreshing showers. Let the river flow and bring life to the all the dry areas of our lives! We need You to sweep over us with all of Your love and wash us with the precious Blood of our Lord and Savior. Let the words of our mouths and the meditation of our hearts be acceptable to You, our Lord and our God! Let everything that has breath praise the Lord. Yes, praise the Lord.

Our Father God has given us His Word. His Word became flesh and lived among us. Our Lord Jesus Christ is that Word. He died on the cross for our sins and rose again. Jesus did this that we might have eternal life and a restored relationship and live forever with Him and our Father God.

Receiving Him (Jesus Christ) we need to understand He is not a God far off but a God at hand! We are His temple and He lives in

us! Yes!! Jesus lives in you and in me! It is not based on how I feel but on His Word!

To them God willed to make known what are the riches of the glory of this mystery among the Gentiles: which is Christ in you, the hope of glory. **Colossians 1:27**

$\mathcal{89}$ STABILITY

Stability can only be found in the Word. This Word, Jesus Christ, lives in us. Jesus Christ living in us is the mystery that Paul talks about in Colossians. To them God willed to make known what are the riches of the glory of the mystery among the Gentiles: which is Christ in you the hope of glory. **Colossians 1:27**

Grab hold. Our Lord Jesus is the solid rock. The journey may be a bit rocky, but our Lord is good and He will bring us safely through. Our footing is secure.

Read daily and receive daily the fresh Bread He has prepared especially for you and me. Get hold of this. In Him we live and move and have our being. The Angel of the Lord encamps around us. We are fully covered. We have assurance from Father God Himself!

$\mathcal{90}$ RELATIONSHIP MORE THAN FEELINGS

Some have commented to me they don't feel as close to God as they have in the past. Feelings themselves are not bad. However, our relationship with Father God is not based on our feelings. Our relationship with Father God is based on His Word to us. His Word is life and His Word to us will never change.

His Word is He has given His Son, Jesus Christ, to die on the cross so that receiving Him You can have eternal life. His Word confirms the death, burial and resurrection of our Lord Jesus Christ. His Word confirms our salvation by telling us when we believe in our hearts Jesus died for our sins and confess with our mouth Jesus is our Lord, we are saved. Again, His Word is truth. Based on our confession of Jesus Christ being our Lord and personal Savior, Father God's Word confirms to us we are saved. That if you confess with your mouth the Lord Jesus and believe in your heart that God has raised Him from the dead, you will be saved. For with the heart one believes unto righteousness, and with the mouth confession is made unto salvation. **Romans 10:9--10**

His Word tells us our Lord Jesus lives in us and we are His temple. Our Lord Jesus living in us couldn't be any closer! No matter how I feel, Jesus lives in me. My high and low feelings will not change God's Word and closeness to me. Yes, Jesus lives in me!

My responsibility is to grow in Him by daily reading His Word and asking Him to guide me and help me to understand. I also need to be in fellowship with Christian brothers and sisters. A Christ-centered church is the best place to have fellowship as often as the doors are open. I look forward to seeing you there.

21 TOUCHED BY HIS PRESENCE IN US

Wherever He entered, into villages, cities, or the country, they laid the sick in the marketplaces, and begged Him that they might just touch the hem of His garment. And as many as touched Him were made well. **Mark 6:56**

The Word of God gives us sight to see spiritually what our Father God wants us to see. Paul tells us in the first chapter of Colossians a mystery that has been revealed to us Gentiles. That mystery is "Christ in us the hope of glory." Our Father God wants us to see and get a hold on this incredible Word! Our Lord Jesus Christ lives in us! We can't be much closer than that! Satan, our enemy, does not want us to see, receive and enter into this holy spiritual reality. The word for receive in the Greek is *lambano*. It is an active verb that means to aggressively take.

Paul fully understood and received this when he said, "It is no longer I that live but Christ lives in me." As I take hold of this reality of my Lord Jesus living in me, everything is fresh and new. I am in continuous touch with my Lord Jesus. I am being transformed moment by moment into what He wants me to be. I am what God says I am in Him. I am made well! This is not a feeling. This is our Father God's Word to you and to me. We are His Body! We are His temple! He lives in you and He lives in me! We are one in Him and He is one in us!! Let us give Him praise! Praise the Lord! Today, this very day, we are made well!

92 HOLY SPIRIT POWER

May our eyes be opened this day to see what the Holy Spirit would speak to us and show us. Anytime fear is involved, we can immediately know this is not from our Father God. Second Timothy comes to mind and we hear Father God's Word to us, "Listen, my child, I have not given you the spirit of fear." This is an awesome Word and brings deliverance. But the Holy Spirit doesn't want us to stop there. There is more. I believe this next part is what He is emphasizing to us for this very day we live. I have been crying out for His power to be released!

Our Lord Jesus showed us, I believe, the answer! He said He could have called for ten thousand angels and they would have come to His aid and defense whenever and however He had need for them to come. Our Lord Jesus did not do this. Our Lord Jesus relied on His Heavenly Father and the Holy Spirit to do what He did. Today I see that is exactly what Father God wants me to do, rely on Him and allow the Holy Spirit in me to do the work. You may be there in your walk and have gotten this.

But I am beginning to understand rather than walking in the form of godliness, we can release the Holy Spirit in us to those around us, as we are directed by the Holy Spirit. We begin walking in the miracle life and demonstration of the power of God in which we are called to walk.

The third and fourth parts of this verse are also essential. We are to walk in His love. We are to do this with a disciplined and sound mind. This means we walk in Him and do this as we listen and are directed to walk by His Word to us through the Holy Spirit!

For God did not give us a spirit of timidity (of cowardice, of craven and cringing and fawning fear), but [He has given us a spirit] of power and of love and of calm and well-balanced mind and discipline and self-control. **Second Timothy 1:7 (AMP)**

Be still, and know that I am God; I will be exalted among the nations, I will be exalted in the earth! **Psalm 46:10**

In all of our busy lives and noise, it is time to just be still! Time out! It is good to just be quiet before the Lord and listen! He will speak. Just be still before Him!

93 STUFF AND MORE STUFF

I am humbled as I am reminded by Father God about how blessed and sheltered I am, and generally speaking, we all are. We are free to do and say pretty much anything we want to.

We have so much we often worry about someone taking our junk. Many people can't leave home because they worry about people coming and getting their valuable stuff. We need to ask, "Do the things we have own us?"

There was a time everything we had would fit in a 1953 Buick. Now it would barely fit in a 3000 sq. ft. home and three sheds and garage. Spoiled beyond spoiled might start to describe this condition. My dear wife has put up with this collector of things for more than fity-five years and she deserves a medal!.

I have justified much of this by saying I might need it someday. Proverbs 16:2 in the Living Bible says, "I can justify everything I do but is God convinced?" It is time to work towards getting back into the 1953 Buick!

In every thing give thanks: for this is the will of God in Christ Jesus concerning you. **First Thessalonians 5:18(KJV)**

94 RECONCILED TO FATHER GOD

We are so blessed and highly favored by our Heavenly Father that His Word tells us, "But as it is written: Eye has not seen, nor ear heard, nor have entered into the heart of man the things which God has prepared for those who love Him." He also tells us, "We shall not live by bread alone but every word that proceeds from the mouth of God." Father God's Word is living. His Son, our Savior, Jesus Christ, is the Word.

Our Lord Jesus tells us in Matthew six, "I am the bread of life. Whoever comes to me will never be hungry again. Whoever believes in me will never be thirsty." As we share the Word we are sharing our Lord Jesus Christ. We are having communion. We are remembering Him and reminding ourselves what He has done for us.

Our relationship with Father God has been restored through our Lord Jesus Christ! Our Father God has come to the garden of our hearts. He is calling, "Where are you?" Let us not be afraid. Our sins are covered by the Blood of our Lord Jesus Christ. Let us answer Him, "Speak, Father God, I am here." As we do this, we will begin to have revealed to us the good plan He has for each of us!

And He took bread, gave thanks and broke it, and gave it to them, saying, "This is My body which is given for you; do this in remembrance of Me. Luke 22:19

95 THE BATTLEFIELD

Understanding the battlefield for us is our mind and what we think, we need to get a hold on what our Father God thinks about us.

How precious it is, Lord, to realize that you are thinking about me constantly! I can't even count how many times a day your thoughts turn toward me. And when I waken in the morning, you are still thinking of me! **Psalm 139:17–18 (TLB)**

Yes, even before the foundation of creation, Father God had us in His mind. That is overwhelming and continues to be so as we realize while we were yet sinners, He sent His Son to die for us. Now that we are His children how much more will He do for us.

I believe our enemy, the Devil, wants us to focus on the mess the world is in and God's judgment, while our Father God wants us to focus on our relationship with Him, His mercy and His grace! Our Father God is not willing that any should perish. With our focus on Father God and feeding on His Word, we have stability. Our anchor grips the Solid Rock, our Lord Jesus Christ.

Our Lord Jesus is our righteousness and we stand in Him. "In Him we live and move and have our being." We share with our words, but even more importantly with our lives, that Jesus Christ is the way, the truth and the life. The result, according to God's

Word, is our family, friends and neighbors will be drawn to Him because He is being lifted up in our lives!

And I, if I be lifted up from the earth, will draw all men unto me. **John 12:32 (KJV)**

96 MAN AFTER GOD'S OWN HEART

Let us receive this fresh Bread for our portion today. I will bless the Lord at all times; His praise shall continually be in my mouth. My soul shall make its boast in the Lord; The humble shall hear of it and be glad. Oh, magnify the Lord with me, And let us exalt His name together. I sought the Lord, and He heard me, And delivered me from all my fears. **Psalm 34:1--4**

Father God tells us David was a man after His own heart. With this understanding of David, we see something when we read Psalm thirty-one. David believed when He asked Father God for His help. He confessed He had it. When Father God tells us we don't have because we don't ask, He is telling us and He wants us to understand that we do have when we ask. We are to believe and confess we have it. In Psalm 31:2 David asks, "Be my rock of refuge, my fortress." In verse three, David confesses having what he asked. Then He says, "You are my rock and my fortress." I am what God says I am. When I speak Father God's Word, I understand I am a conduit for His Word. His Word will not return void!

In You, O Lord, I put my trust; Let me never be ashamed; Deliver me in Your righteousness. Bow down Your ear to me, Deliver me speedily; Be my rock of refuge, A fortress of defense to save me. For You are my rock and my fortress; Therefore, for Your name's sake Lead me and guide me. **Psalm 31:1--3**

97 IS GOD CONVINCED

Father God's Word tells me I can justify everything I do, but then the question becomes, with all of my reasoning, is my Father God convinced?

All the ways of a man are pure in his own eyes, But the Lord weighs the spirits. **Proverbs 16:2**

98 GRANDFATHER'S KEY

I have an old skeleton key. The key belonged to my grandfather who died before I was born. Where I lived in Indiana, this key would unlock any door in my neighborhood and most doors in our town. What is more interesting, even with locks and keys the doors on most homes were not locked.

This was the case until the 1950's. It is heart-breaking to see what has happened to our country! As God's people we need to seek our God.

Father God, I need you. My neighborhood, my city, my state, my country and the world needs you. Your Word tells me You have and will provide a way when there seems to be no way. You have told me, "Pray and do not faint." You have told me, "Ask." You have told me as your child, "Humble yourself and pray." I know You hear me and I know you care more than I can imagine. You are not deaf. Your arm has not been shortened. You alone can satisfy the needs from the smallest to the largest and You are mighty to perform all you have promised. I believe the windows of Heaven are open. You have told me to boldly come into your presence. You have dipped Your scepter to me and bid me to come. I come. I am asking for forgiveness and mercy. I need You. We need You. God is our refuge and strength, A very present help in trouble. **Psalm 46:1**

$\mathcal{99}$ SPEAK THE TRUTH

Our Heavenly Father speaks to us through His Word and tells us to speak the truth in love. In the world around us, lying is commonplace. Our courts have ruled lying is a part of politics. How often do we hear, "Honestly speaking," or, "Honestly?" This should not be necessary. Every time we speak it should be the truth!

Neighbors lie to each other, speaking with flattering lips and deceitful hearts. **Psalm 12:2 (NLT)**

Therefore, putting away lying, "Let each one of you speak truth with his neighbor," for we are members of one another. **Ephesians 4:25**

100 WAR ROOM

Yesterday we watched the movie WAR ROOM. If you haven't yet viewed this movie, please do. All of us in the Body of Christ are engaged in battle. We need to contend for our marriages, our children, our grandchildren, our friends and our neighbors. Our micro church is our home. "Where two or more are gathered I am in their midst," says the Lord. The gates of hell shall not prevail against this church! As priests called of God, we need to contend and stand in the gap called and equipped by our Father God. We need to enter our war rooms and seek His face!

Beloved, while I was very diligent to write to you concerning our common salvation, I found it necessary to write to you exhorting you to contend earnestly for the faith which was once for all delivered to the saints. **Jude 3**

101 BELIEVE THE WORD AND WALK IN IT

Father God gives His promises, all of which are amen and yes in Christ Jesus. Then He permits us to be tested to see if we will wait on Him to do what He has promised. Let us listen and hear Father God's still, small voice. His Word is truth and life and His reward is certain. Nothing can separate us from His love and He will complete the work He has begun in us. Let us this day believe His Word and walk in it, no matter what is going on around us or happening to us!

Oh, let the wickedness of the wicked come to an end, But establish the just; For the righteous God tests the hearts and minds. **Psalm 7:9**

The Lord tests the righteous, But the wicked and the one who loves violence His soul hates. **Psalm 11:5**

No temptation has overtaken you except such as is common to man; but God is faithful, who will not allow you to be tempted beyond what you are able, but with the temptation will also make the way of escape, that you may be able to bear it. **First Corinthians 10:13**

Blessed is the man who endures temptation; for when he has been approved, he will receive the crown of life which the Lord has promised to those who love Him. **James 1:12**

102 I AM WHAT FATHER GOD SAYS I AM

Our Father God wants us this day to understand we are what He says we are. This means as I believe in my heart and confess with my mouth so I am. I am saved. I am healed. I am a child of God. I am strong. I am redeemed. I am an ambassador of the Lord my God and He has given me His authority and supports and backs every Word I speak in His Name. His Word will not return void. Father God, as your children and your family, let us understand and enter into what You have established through our Lord Jesus Christ for us even now this day.

And has made us kings and priests to His God and Father, to Him be glory and dominion forever and ever. Amen. **Revelation 1:6**

And have made us kings and priests to our God; And we shall reign on the earth. **Revelation 5:10**

103 WAITING ON THE LORD

Waiting in our world for anything today is almost unheard of. The world says, "Why wait when you can have it now?" Many cannot sit or stand and be still. They have to move. Rest escapes many people. Many of us have to take a pill in order to get any sleep. All of this is evidence of our need for our Heavenly Father and His provisions for us. His Words to us are, "Wait." "Stand." "Come unto me and find rest for your souls." His Word tells us, "Obedience is better than sacrifice." It is time for us to listen, receive and obey His Living Word to us. The best thing we can do is wait on the Lord. Be still and listen for His Word for this day. We start by taking a few minutes as we begin our day and just ask Him to speak to us and help us. Read a chapter in Proverbs. Our brief prayer and reading might take all of five minutes, but in doing this, good things will begin to be evidenced in our lives. Why? Because our Heavenly Father has promised when we acknowledge Him in all our ways He will direct our paths.

104 ANSWERS TO PRAYER

Now this is the confidence that we have in Him, that if we ask anything according to His will, He hears us. And if we know that He hears us, whatever we ask, we know that we have the petitions that we have asked of Him. **First John 5:14--15**

John is teaching us about God's will and our prayers. When we pray according to God's will, God hears and we know we have what we have prayed for. Our Father God is not deaf and all of His promises are yes and amen in Christ Jesus. Derek Prince, in his book, SHAPING HISTORY THROUGH PRAYER AND FASTING, tells us, "The present tense 'we have' does not necessarily indicate an immediate manifestation of the thing we prayed for, but it does indicate an immediate assurance that the thing is already granted to us by God." He goes on to say, "This agrees with the teaching of Mark 11:24, Therefore I say to you, whatever things you ask when you pray, believe that you receive them, and you will have them. **Receiving comes at the very moment of praying. After that, the actual manifestation of that which we have received follows at the appropriate time."**

105 VICTORY IN JESUS

As we begin this new day, let us understand we are not wrestling against flesh and blood. We are in a spiritual battle. Let us get dressed for it. Let us put on the helmet of salvation, the breastplate of righteousness, the belt of truth, the gospel of peace shoes, and pick up the shield of faith and the sword of the Spirit.

Let us pray: Heavenly Father, bless me indeed, expand my territory and my sphere of influence. Keep Your Holy Spirit presence upon me. Deliver me from the evil one. Heavenly Father, be glorified in the process of all I do today. In Jesus' mighty name, amen. Our Lord Jesus has given us the victory.

Let us walk in it, praying as we go through our day in the Spirit with a thankful heart. Yes, our Lord Jesus has given us the victory.

106 TEN COMMANDMENTS

We are living in a time when everyone does pretty much what they want to do. People don't want anyone telling them what to do. After all, who knows better what to do than I do? In our culture there are no absolutes. These absolutes, The Ten Commandments, were taught at home and reinforced at school. The home and family have been under serious attack. Conditions are far from anything like it was seventy years ago.

Today with no Ten Commandments to live by, people can do and are doing whatever they feel like doing. After all, if it feels good, it's probably okay! Why can't we see what is wrong? We need, I need, to repent and cry out to our loving Heavenly Father for forgiveness and turn from my selfish ways. I want to have my Lord Jesus as King and Lord of my life. Choose today whom you will serve. As for me and my house, we will serve the Lord. In those days there was no king in Israel. Everyone did what was right in his own eyes. **Judges 17:6(ESV)**

107 PAINFUL LOSS

I was eight. My dad had been in bed for a month after his surgery. Janice Louise, my four-and-a-half- year-old sister suddenly became very ill. By evening Mom and Dad, after calling our family doctor, left with my sister to meet the doctor at the hospital in the nearby town where we lived. My aunt was at our home to make sure I was not alone and to get me off to school the next day. At about ten o'clock in the morning while I was in school, I knew my sister wasn't coming home. About an hour later our pastor and my Dad came through the door of the second grade of our country school. Without them saying anything, I knew I wouldn't see my sister again this side of Heaven.

As hard as it was for me, it was even harder for my parents. I am telling this because even in our family I don't think anyone has ever heard what happened. My Mom and Dad have now both joined Janice in Heaven along with many other family members, including my Uncle Clarence who was killed on a Salerno, Italy, beachhead two years earlier during WWII. I witnessed my Mom's and my Dad's grief for my uncle and then my sister.

The next day my sister's body lay in a casket in our living room. I can remember going from my bedroom out to the living room. I stood alone in the night looking at the open casket holding my sister's body. There was one lamp standing at the head and another at the foot of her casket. A week later after my sister's funeral, I wanted to just go and hide in my room and never come out into the light again. I felt guilty for her death. I thought if I had treated my sister better she wouldn't have died. Self-pity is deadly no matter the age.

Why am I sharing this? Because the battlefield we all deal with is our minds. We must understand the enemy is a liar. He wants us to think no one around us has ever gone through anything close to our situation. First of all, our Lord Jesus personally carried every heartache, sorrow, sickness, mess, you-name-it. All of these were laid on Him. He bore all of this for you and me. Our burden, whatever it is, He wants us to give to Him. Addictions, actual guilt, guilt feelings, again you-name-it, give it to Him.

Also when we really get to know each other, we soon learn most around us have lived through very difficult if not impossible seeming times. Some of you are currently suffering and grieving, and when you look at those around you and as they share what are intended to be comforting words, the thought you have is they don't understand. Let's say they don't, but many around you love Jesus and He lives in them. Jesus always understands. They love Jesus and they love you. He speaks to them and out of obedience they reach out to you to share words of encouragement and love they have heard and received from our Heavenly Father to share with you and me. Let us receive what they share as an act of love for us and love for our Lord Jesus. Then if what is being shared is less than this, it is God's problem and He will deal with them. Because of His love in us, we do not keep a record of any offense we may experience. We are free from any sin that might so easily be picked up and carried if we were to choose to do so.

108 FATHER GOD IS GOOD

The story of my sister and her homegoing was something I believe needed to be shared because there are some who recently or not so recently experienced the homegoing of their precious loved one. Sometimes I hear, "How long will the heartache last?" The heartache, I am sure, varies with each of us left behind but for me after nearly seventy-five years there are still emotional moments. Our loved ones are not to be forgotten. Our hope is in our Heavenly Father and His Son Jesus Christ. The Holy Spirit is our Comforter and He gives us what we need to make it one day at a time.

With my sister's homegoing, Dad, Mom and I had some very difficult times. Several weeks after Janice had gone home, I remember when Dad held my Mom and I while we all three wept. This is what we need to understand, Mom and Dad trusted God. They prayed.

About a year after my sister died I accepted Jesus as my Lord and Savior. I am still a work in process. Without God I honestly don't know how anyone can make it through these times. He is there for us and He wants more than we can imagine to help us make it through.

Mom and Dad never blamed God. God did not cause my sister's death. Mom and Dad were always thankful and considered my sister and I as having been loaned to them from God. My mother shared at my sister's funeral about "The Little Girl God Loaned to Me." I would share with you this scripture at this point. "All things work together for good for them that love God and are called according to His purpose." This promise is for all of us.

For my mother to have another child would require somewhat of a miracle because of some health issues she was dealing with and her age at the time. But again God loves His children and is always there to help when they ask Him. My parents, had this not happened, most likely would not have had my brother. God knew all of us before we were even thought of, no matter how we were born, in or out of marriage. We have always been an important part of His creation. Each of us is priceless.

All the money in the world could not purchase salvation for even one of us. And yet our Lord Jesus paid the full price for all of us. God heard Mom, Dad and I as we prayed for a baby. A baby, not to replace Janice, but because they truly wanted another child as wonderful as I might have been. Please feel free to laugh and if you know me, you will laugh without any prompting.

They wanted another child and God knew my brother was destined for our family. My brother, Jerry Wayne, was born about two years after Janice Louise went home. Jerry Wayne Carlson was a delight, joy and comfort to my parents as soon as he was born. My brother was a large part of the good from God that came from the difficulty of Janice going home so very early in her life.

I pray you who are hurting right now will receive. This receive means to take comfort from the Comforter. Holy Spirit, I ask You right now to touch all reading this with Your presence. Their eyes are the windows to their hearts. Touch and release Your comfort. Give them Your peace, Your hope and breathe Your comfort on them along with new life. In Jesus' mighty name, amen.

109 GOD'S PLAN

As a nation it would seem that many want to give control of wellness plans or health care to the government. With control the government, ultimately, will determine who lives and who dies. I heard a worldly man on the radio today say, "The government understands if they control the wellness or health care plans they can control the people." No one cares about your and my well-being more than our Heavenly Father cares. Our Lord Jesus paid the full price to make us whole spiritually and physically. In the Old Testament He made a covenant with His children, "If you will love Me and keep My commandments I will not put any of these sicknesses or diseases upon you."

As New Testament believers and His children, we have an even better covenant. In the new covenant we have forgiveness for all our sins and we have healing for all our sicknesses and diseases. By the Blood of our Lord Jesus we are forgiven and cleansed and by His stripes we are healed. Our unbelief will keep us from realizing any and all of these promises of our Heavenly Father. Not wanting to wait on the Lord goes along with unbelief. Heavenly Father, I want to walk in Your Truth. Your Word is truth. I want to walk in Your deliverance and salvation, spiritually and physically. Your plan, Heavenly Father, is better than any government plan! I choose Your plan, Heavenly Father!

110 COME TO THE GARDEN

Our Lord Jesus has restored the Garden of Eden experience for us with our Heavenly Father. I come to the garden alone. Be still and listen. My purpose is to hear from Father God. The garden experience can happen anywhere and anytime. How can this be? It is possible because the garden is in my heart. Hide God's Word in my heart, you ask? The answer in God's Word to us is what King David said in Psalm 119, "Thy Word have I hid in my heart that I might not sin against thee."

God's Word says I will know His voice. So as I stand quietly in the garden, I hear the still, small voice of Father God speaking and answering the questions that I have. He speaks simply and directly. One of the most sought after questions is, "Who am I?" Many take off and literally go around the world to find themselves. They go to all the world's religions and try all sorts of mind-altering avenues in their attempt to find themselves.

What is the answer I hear from God concerning the question, "Who am I?" This is the response I hear from Father God, "You are who I say you are." Yes, I am a child of God. I am who He says I am.

///// INSECURITY

Anyone who says they have not had to deal with insecurity is probably not being honest. Our Heavenly Father who made us and knew us before we were even conceived knows all of our insecurities and our related issues. He wants us to know we are secure in Him. Our security comes from our Heavenly Father. Our Lord Jesus, His Son, is the rock of security. By faith we are anchored in that Rock! Know this, we are secure in our Lord Jesus Christ.

Proverbs tells us His Name is a strong tower and the righteous run into it and are safe. Our Heavenly Father gives us confirmation of our security in more than seventy verses throughout His Word to us. We are more than conquerors through Him! For example, in Romans we learn that nothing can separate us from His love. The eternal God is a dwelling place, And underneath are the everlasting arms. **Deuteronomy 33:27. You and I are secure in our Lord Jesus Christ. He is in the boat with us! He will never leave or forsake us. He is a friend that stays closer than a brother.**

112 A LITTLE TALK WITH GOD

As we face the issues of our daily lives, whom do we go to for help? Is our first act to talk to Father God about the matter? Or is it to try to fix it ourselves as we go with our issues to every place or person we think can help or solve the problem? Then in the course of our efforts in order to cover the bases, do we ask for prayer and then perhaps even pray ourselves? If you were the Creator of the universe and you had given provision for every need of your creation and all they had to do was believe and ask you to help and they went everywhere else instead of coming to you, how would you feel about that?

Father God, no matter what, help me to believe Your Words to me and Your promises for satisfying my every need. Help me to choose always to come to You first, to believe so that I can receive the very best there is, your provision! In Jesus' mighty name, help me! You alone are God and I run to You this day! Paul tells me in Philippians four my Heavenly Father will supply my every need through Christ Jesus. The faith walk is foolishness to the world. I choose the walk of faith. What will you choose? the Lord is saying, "Don't be rebellious. Come to me for your advice, direction and needs." More often than not we go everywhere but to our Heavenly Father. Woe to the rebellious children," says the Lord, "Who take counsel, but not of Me, And who devise plans, but not of My Spirit, That they may add sin to sin. **Isaiah 30:1**

113 POWER OF GOD

Jesus is the way, the truth and the life. No one comes to the Father but through Him! The gospel message is foolishness to the world, but to those of us who are being saved, it is the power of God. Our Bible tells us we overcome the enemy by the Blood of the Lamb and the word of our testimony. Without the shedding of blood there is no remission of sin.

Jesus' shed Blood once and for all broke our sin curse and set us free. It was at the cross where I first saw the Light! All my burdens rolled away. What can make me whole again, nothing but the Blood of Jesus. Oh, precious is the flow that makes me whiter than snow. If we want to see the power of God, we need to preach Jesus Christ crucified, buried and resurrected! The signs and wonders will follow the message of the cross. Our Heavenly Father has promised! He does what He promises!

114 IN HIS PRESENCE

Let us quiet ourselves before the throne of our Heavenly Father. He has instructed us to come boldly into His presence. Let us enter in and be still before Him. In this stillness as we are quiet before Him, we can hear His still, small voice. His Words are truth and life.

As we are still and listening, He reveals Himself to us and we know according to His Word this is God our Heavenly Father. In His presence there is no condemnation. His peace and His joy fill us to overflowing. His love fills our hearts and in this quietness we receive His strength and confidence that nothing is impossible. With a thankful heart we bow before Him and worship Him, Lord of lords and King of kings. We worship and adore You, bowing down before You, songs of praises singing, hallelujahs ringing. Yes, this is our song, praising our Savior all the day long!

115 OIL FOR OUR LAMP

The promises of our Heavenly Father are certain and sure. The journey to enter in and receive the fulfillment of the promise may be neither short nor quick. Without faith it is impossible to please our Heavenly Father God. Faith comes by hearing and hearing by the Word. To enter in and receive the fulfillment we need the Word. The Word is the oil for our lamp. The lamp provides light for our journey so we can see the path. Without the oil, we will become discouraged and give in to the circumstances.

This is what the old song we used to sing told us, "Give me oil in my lamp, keep me burning, burning until the break of day." God's Word tells us, "Weeping may endure for the night but joy comes in the morning." Don't give up. Our dawn is about to break! Our Lord Jesus is right here in the boat with us! We will see the break of day!

116 HEALING MIRACLE

Heavenly Father, Your Word is greater than any other word. Your Word is life. Let it be, Lord Jesus. Let it be in me. I love Your Word. You are the Word. About two weeks ago, I listened to a teaching by a pastor who shared what we fear will become our God. Because we fear death, we have put our trust in the medical profession. We must know what we have. After all, I have a pain or a twinge of sorts. There must be something wrong. I go to the doctor for a diagnosis and tests to find out what I have. The doctor will tell me and even tell me if what I have is terminal and how long I am expected to live. I have seen this in my life and the life of friends and family.

Twelve years ago I received a phone call telling me the caller's three-year-old nephew was in a children's hospital with spinal meningitis and would not live the night. The Holy Spirit spoke and said, "Tell this child's mother God's Word is greater than the doctor's word. This child shall live." Then the doctors said if this child does live he will be a vegetable and a quadruple amputee. This child lives and is normal today. Yes, this was a miracle. Our God lives. His Word is greater than any other word. He is the same yesterday, today and forever. His Word is life and will not return void.

I choose God's Word and with the help of the Holy Spirit and His presence, choose this day to walk in it! God is my Hope and

Refuge. He is my Healer and I am His child. No weapon of the enemy formed against me will prosper. I am called to share the good news, salvation spiritually and physically! We are to go and come when our Heavenly Father says so. I choose to listen to my Heavenly Father. We also believe in our heart and confess with our mouth we are healed.

Is anyone among you sick? He must call for the elders (spiritual leaders) of the church and they are to pray over him, anointing him with [a]oil in the name of the Lord; and the prayer of faith will restore the one who is sick, and the Lord will raise him up; and if he has committed sins, he will be forgiven. **James 5:14--15 (AMP)**

117 GOD'S PROMISED HEALING

We can miss our promise of healing or blessing because we don't understand the Word. First, we need to understand who is making the promise. Our Creator, God Himself, is making the promise. He is giving us His Word. He cannot lie. I believe our problem is understanding not all healing is instantaneous. All healing is from God. There is the instant miracle healing and then healing over time.

When we pray and the symptoms are still there and we don't see an immediate change, then we decide our Heavenly Father doesn't want to heal us or it is not His will. When we do this, we are not believing. We must believe no matter what our senses are telling us. It is the prayer of faith that makes the difference. We can trust our Heavenly Father. All of His promises are yes and amen! He will do what He has promised. Just as when we accept Jesus as our personal Savior we believe in our heart and confess with our mouth, we also believe in our heart and confess with our mouth we are healed.

Is anyone among you sick? He must call for the elders (spiritual leaders) of the church and they are to pray over him, anointing him with [a]oil in the name of the Lord; and the prayer of faith will restore the one who is sick, and the Lord will raise him up; and if he has committed sins, he will be forgiven. **James 5:14—15(AMP)**

My family heritage has been to take ownership of sicknesses. My cold, my measles, my strep throat, my broken nose, my broken leg, my broken arm, my concussion, my oh my, and the list goes on!

Then about four years ago, I heard this question asked of me by the Holy Spirit, "Why do you want to take ownership of any sickness or disease?" In our culture at the first sign of any discomfort, the questions erupt! "What do I have? Have you been to a doctor? What was the doctor's diagnosis?" Then as soon as I say, "I have_____," I have taken ownership.

As I began to respond to the Holy Spirit's question by asking Father God about this, I began to learn sicknesses are not from God. According to John 10:10, our enemy, the evil one, has come only to steal, and to kill, and to destroy! Our Lord Jesus has come that we would have life and life abundantly. Jesus is my Healer! In Psalm 103:3 He tells me He has healed all my sicknesses. I have surrendered all sickness ownership. I plead the Blood of Jesus no matter how I feel! I don't own any sicknesses anymore. My Lord Jesus has set me free! Yes, it is a battle. The victory has been won! I am well and I am free indeed. My Lord Jesus has set me free! As a child of God, I go to Him as a child. His child and forever I am! I believe and I receive! Amazing grace! There's room at the cross for you and me! The healing stream still flows!

118 JESUS PAID IT ALL

Thinking about our precious Lord Jesus and what He did and continues to do is beyond amazing. He willingly gave His life for You and me. He opened not His mouth or hinted in any way He would resist the course that had been set before Him. He was committed to our redemption. Every sin, every sickness, every hurt, and every pain was laid on Him. He freely bore it all. The suffering and shame He bore words cannot begin to describe nor can they begin to tell. As our sins, yours and mine, were laid on Him, Father God, seeing all this sin, turned a deaf ear to His beloved Son.

Yes, our Lord Jesus has paid it all. All to Him I owe. It's here at the cross, along with the thief at His side, I find deliverance and new life. The Blood, His Blood, cleanses my every sin. His stripes give me health and deliverance from every sickness and disease. Oh, how I love Him. I will ever live and serve Him, Jesus my Lord. Oh, how I love Jesus because he first loved me. I took Jesus as my Savior, You take Him. too. Oh, what a Savior! Who forgives all your sins, Who heals all your diseases. **Psalm 103:3 (AMP)**

119 THE BLOOD COVERING

What can make me whole again? The Blood of Jesus washes my every sin and every stain. My Lord Jesus has made me whole. He touched me and I will never be the same. There is wonder-working power in the Blood. Our enemy, the Devil, is overcome by the Blood of the Lamb. He sees we are covered by the Blood of Jesus. He has to pass over us. Yes, there is a fountain that flows from the veins of our Lord Jesus. It is here at the cross where I first saw the Light and every burden of my heart rolled away. The Blood of my Lord Jesus covers me and I plead the Blood over my family and friends.

Our Lord Jesus is calling for us to choose to stay under His Blood covering. The world around us doesn't even want the mention of His name let alone the mention of His Blood. Yes, there is victory for each of us as we plead the Blood of Jesus over our lives and proclaim to those around us that our Lord Jesus lives. Yes, our testimony and His shed Blood gives us victory! Victory in Jesus!

But if we [really] walk in the Light [that is, live each and every day in conformity with the precepts of God], as He Himself is in the Light, we have [true, unbroken] fellowship with one another [He with us, and we with Him], and the blood of Jesus His Son cleanses us from all sin [by erasing the stain of sin, keeping us cleansed from sin in all its forms and manifestations **First John 1:7 (AMP)**

ABOUT THE AUTHOR

I have had a personal relationship with my Heavenly Father (God) for 71 years. This relationship started when I was eight years old. My relationship has become more personal and more real each year. I have read the Bible through 25 times in the last 19 years.

In addition to personal study and Bible reading, I have memorized the Word and continue to memorize the Word because the Word is life to me. I have attended Wheaton College and Moody Bible Institute where I studied the Bible. I have taught adult Sunday School for more than five years and led weekly men's Bible studies for more than 20 years. I have done lay preaching for many years.

My Bible tells me I am a friend of God. As a friend of God I have been led to write the devotions that are shared in this book to share with other friends of God and any other person that might desire to have a more personal relationship with our Heavenly Father. What qualifies me more than anything else is that I believe I have been called of God to write this book.

I honorably served in the US army. With the help of the GI Bill I was able to go to school. I received a bachelor's degree in mechanical engineering. I worked for 30 years for Weyerhaeuser Company and was promoted to Director of the Wood Products Maintenance in that company. I am now retired from Weyerhaeuser. I am happy and blessed to be married to my wife Susan for 56+ years. We have three married sons and nine grandchildren. I have traveled nearly around the world.

We currently live on a small five-acre farm bordering the state of Washington's Lake Terrell Wildlife Refuge. I grow Christmas trees, garden, grow flowers and feed a lot of birds. I love to fish and to share the Word of God.

Printed in the United States
By Bookmasters